EVANGELIZATION IN THE CULTURE AND SOCIETY OF THE UNITED STATES AND THE BISHOP AS TEACHER OF THE FAITH

Meeting of His Holiness John Paul II with the Archbishops of the United States

MARCH 8–11, 1989

ISBN 1-55586-278-0

Contents

Appendices

Opening Comments
by Joseph Cardinal Bernardin

It is a privilege for me to speak in the name of my brother cardinals and archbishops from the United States on the occasion of this historic and important meeting. In their name and my own, I would like to express our deepest gratitude to our Holy Father, Pope John Paul II, who has so graciously offered this opportunity to us. It is one more expression of his often-demonstrated love for the Church in the United States. We are also grateful to his principal collaborators, the members of the Roman Curia, for their diligent efforts in assisting the Holy Father and the bishops throughout the world in the pastoral care of the people entrusted to them.

This particular meeting is a follow-up to the Holy Father's visit to the United States in 1987 and the bishops' *Ad Limina* visits to Rome in 1988. All of these visits, in which cordial, candid exchanges take place, have helped to bridge the physical distance between the Church in the United States and the Church in Rome; they facilitate better communications.

The overall theme of this meeting is *evangelization*. Each particular Church is called to evangelize, to proclaim the universal message of Jesus' redeeming love as handed on by the Church in a specific cultural context. We, on our part, as teachers of the faith, proclaim that Gospel in a different and, at times, difficult set of circumstances.

The United States is blessed in many ways: with plentiful resources, with cherished freedoms, with extraordinary opportunities. We proclaim the Gospel in a communications-oriented society in a world that has become ever smaller. Because of the freedom of speech and the freedom of press inherent in our society, and because of the importance accorded to the Church within the United States by our fellow Americans, discussions that at one time might have been considered intramural have significant repercussions throughout the world. We work out our destiny in full view of the public's eye. This is an element of our ministry that we are

1

not always able to control. Perhaps this is a special blessing of our experience—although some would see it as a mixed blessing.

Measured as the world measures, our country is numbered among the "superpowers" with all that that implies in terms of responsibility. Measured as a pilgrim people, Americans are described as being among the most actively "religious" in the world, while wrestling with the universal problem of secularism which can be a major obstacle to the full acceptance of *religious* responsibility.

There are certain aspects of the American character that have been fashioned during the 213 years of our nation's existence. Americans are accustomed to "government in the open," that is, most of our institutions debate and decide the major issues in public with maximum participation by the governors and those governed. Americans are accustomed to electing their public officials and those who will actualize their noblest hopes and aspirations. Americans are accustomed to exercising their basic freedoms by civil discourse, open to inquiry into any issue that touches upon the common good or the rights of the individual.

As U.S. bishops, we value highly the founding principles of our country and its democratic traditions. Freedom of religion, the absence of an established church, and the resulting religious pluralism have benefited our Church and, indeed, all churches and religious faiths. While, as a faith community, we operate according to different principles both in terms of our teaching and governance, I do not see these freedoms or their exercise as being in conflict with our faithfulness to the universal Catholic tradition that is ours. Rather, they constitute a significant dimension of the *context* in which our Catholic community exists, the Gospel is preached, and our commitment to our universal tradition is espoused. Our experiences, like those of every national hierarchy, are rooted in that dual reality: the Gospel which is universal and one as proclaimed in a particular cultural and societal setting. It is important that we share these experiences with our Holy Father and his advisers, just as it is important that the pope, as pastor of the universal Church, and his advisers share with us their convictions and insights from the perspective of the universal Church. While this is not an action-oriented meeting, we will begin here this evening what the Holy Father has called a new form of dialogue between the successor of St. Peter and those successors of the apostles who minister in the United States.

2

What is it, then, that we, the archbishops of the United States, bring to this dialogue?

While we make no claim to being the biggest or the best, structurally we speak for a Church that encompasses some 53 million of the faithful. We have a rich history of evangelization and of education. We have the largest privately supported school system. There are more Catholic colleges and universities in the United States than elsewhere. We have built upon the shoulders of great leaders of the past—and we are proud of that accomplishment. We have a long and glorious history of committed service to the poor, the abandoned, the marginalized, and the needy through highly organized charitable and service programs. We enjoy a Catholic health system which for years has been known for the highest standards of professionalism and Christlike care for the sick and poor.

The bishops of the United States have addressed many social, ethical, and moral issues of both national and worldwide import from the perspective of our Catholic heritage, providing guidance for our people as they confront these realities. In that context, I would make special mention of our National Conference of Catholic Bishops, which has enabled us to discuss important issues pertaining to the Church's life when these issues are best addressed in a collaborative manner and do not impose in any way on the authority of the local bishop.

Finally, we are blessed with many dedicated, hardworking priests, deacons, and men and women religious. Together with our laity, they are the incarnation of the Church in our time and place. In a special way, it is they who represent what we would bring to this dialogue. For beyond the institutional structures I have outlined above, it is the clergy, religious, and faithful who reflect the experience of a local Church which has striven to implement the renewal called for by the Second Vatican Council. This post-conciliar era has been a time of ferment within the universal Church—reflecting the experience of past centuries when important events like councils have taken place in the Church. This is true also of our experience in the United States. But, notwithstanding the ferment and, at times, the polarities, we share the Holy Father's conviction that not only was the Second Vatican Council the work of the Holy Spirit, but so too are these times of the continued implementation of the Council's wisdom and directives. It is an era sometimes marked with strain, but also with growth and renewal.

We come, then, to this city of Sts. Peter and Paul, a place so special to our faith. We come to Christ's vicar on earth to share stories—the stories of our stewardship and our people. We come to tell of the difficulties and challenges we face, but also of the faith- and hope-filled people whom we are privileged to love and serve. We come to speak but also to listen, to pray together, to learn together, and to go forth again renewed—incorporated in that visible source and sign of unity whom we call and who is indeed our pontiff and father.

May the discussions of these next several days make us open to the promptings of the Holy Spirit so that we may be ever more diligent and effective as we go about the Lord's worship.

Opening Address
by His Holiness John Paul II

Dear Brothers in the Episcopate,

I am particularly happy to welcome you, the metropolitans of the United States, and with you my co-workers in the Roman Curia, on the occasion of this special assembly. This historic meeting which begins today is an opportunity to give a clearer expression to the bonds of ecclesial and ministerial communion which unite us. We already know each other well, since one of the first pastoral visits of my pontificate was to the United States in 1979. During that visit I was able to learn a great deal about the Church in your country: I had a chance to listen to and observe, to speak and pray with the people of the East and Midwest. In 1983 you came to Rome on your *Ad Limina* visits and I had the opportunity of learning more about your work. In 1987 I was pleased to accept your kind invitation to make my second visit to the United States, this time concentrating on the regions of the South and West. And finally, last year you came again for your *Ad Limina* visits, during which time we reflected once more on aspects of our common pastoral mission.

Thus on several occasions in the past, I had the opportunity to express my gratitude for the way in which the Church in the United States, and particularly you, its pastors, welcomed my visits there, as well as to manifest my appreciation of your pastoral zeal as I received each of you individually. At this time, I would like to voice again those same sentiments.

Today, then, dear brothers, as we continue our journey of faith together, I welcome you who are here precisely because of the office you hold. As metropolitans you are in a special position to represent and to express the concerns of the particular churches in your country.

We have come together to consider important matters regarding ecclesial life in the United States. Our gathering is the continuation of an exchange, a truly open exchange, which aims to strengthen our *partnership in the Gospel*. We do so with an organic view of our mission as bishops in mind, a view which "must take into account the perennial exigencies of the Gospel; it must also express the indisputable priorities of the life of the Church today, both in her universal needs and in the special requirements of the Church in the United States. At the same time it must faithfully reflect *the call of the Second Vatican Council to reform and renewal*" (*Ad Limina* address of May 31, 1988).

At the heart of our concern is "Evangelization in the Context of the Culture and Society of the United States, with Particular Emphasis on the Role of the Bishop as Teacher of the Faith." From the outset, I would ask you to discuss the urgent task of evangelization from the perspective of the bishop as *teacher of the faith*. In this precise context, you are invited to reflect on the agents, methods, and beneficiaries of evangelization. Your mission as authentic teachers of the faith has as its purpose the building up of the Body of Christ. You, united with the Bishop of Rome, are the pillars upon which rests all the work of evangelization. Hence the strength and vitality of the local church depend to a great extent on the steadfastness of your faith, hope, and love.

As Pastor of the Universal Church, I wish to *encourage you in your ministry*. I am fully conscious of the challenges you face in bringing the gospel message to a world that does not often readily accept it. Your people experience the difficulties of being Christians in today's world. Yet at the same time they search for direction in following the path marked out by Christ. In these days together we shall attempt to clarify *our own vision* of where the Lord wishes to lead us and his people as we stand on the threshold of the third millennium of Christianity. We can be confident in the outcome of our efforts because we know that the Lord of the vineyard is in our midst. He is the one who has chosen us as his servants to carry out the mission of evangelization. In the words of Saint Paul, we have been "set apart for the Gospel of God . . . the Gospel concerning his Son" (Rom 1:1,3). As such, we accept his call and we do so joyfully. But we do not hesitate to turn to him in prayer for greater strength and guidance. This is why all our discussions will be placed in the context of prayer and will culminate in our celebration of the Eucharist together at the tomb of Saint Peter.

Let us go forward then, invoking the powerful intercession of Mary Immaculate and trusting in the knowledge that the Lord is ready to assist us in our pastoral endeavors, for he has sent us his Spirit to be with us and to guide us in all truth and love. Dear brothers: *In the power of the Holy Spirit* let us continue to make every effort to assist all the Catholic people of the United States to proclaim by *the holiness of their lives* that "Jesus Christ is Lord" (Eph 2:11).

Response to the Holy Father by Archbishop John May

Most Holy Father, you have favored us with words of welcome, with words of encouragement, with words of advice—and we are grateful. We have come many miles from our own dioceses, yet we feel that we are home. Home is where family dwells, where love lives—and we feel that here. You are our father in Jesus Christ, and we have a keen sense of your love for each of us.

In September of 1987, you graced our shores with your presence and our spirits with your words. Throughout the past year, when we came to Rome for our *Ad Limina* visits, we felt the warmth of your hospitality, the strength of your support. Now you have blessed us again by inviting us here to talk with you and with your Curia collaborators as a summation of your visit to us and of our own visits to you.

We come, 33 metropolitan bishops representing almost 400 Roman Catholic bishops of the United States and over 53 million Catholics who people our land. Several weeks ago, you wrote to us bishops, announcing that our teaching role in evangelization would be the theme of these conversations. That theme struck us as welcome and wise. It is rooted, of course, in the word for "Gospel," and that word was the title of a popular musical play in America some years back. It called us to see Jesus more clearly, love him more dearly, follow him more nearly, day by day, day by day. To help people do that is our work of evangelization both for those who share our faith and for those who are unchurched.

No one knows more about spreading the Gospel than you do, Holy Father. In your work here in Rome, and in your missionary journeys around the world, you have carried the good news of Jesus—in a courageous and loving way. We are here to learn from you. But we are also here to speak to you as you have invited us to do. We are your brother bishops, linked with you in the love of the Lord. And so we want to share—with you and with your fellow servants here in Rome—what we are seeing and hearing as we walk the streets of our land.

9

May I speak, then, of the cultural context in which we live and work? There are several elements of that ambiance which impact our work directly, and I will list them before I explain: The United States is pluralistic; it enjoys total religious liberty; organized religion abounds in America; there is full freedom of thought; and the spirit of democracy runs strong. Perhaps it might help if I comment briefly on each of these factors.

First, the *pluralism*. On the same street in America, you may have living side by side: a black Baptist family with roots in Africa; a Cambodian couple who fled Indochina with their Buddhist faith intact; a Jewish family who came to escape discrimination in the Soviet Union; Polish and Latin American refugees seeking a home in the local Catholic parish. That street, for all of its bewildering diversity, is the typical strength of America. Our coins tell of the American experiment—*E pluribus unum*—to fashion one nation from many diverse people. It is an experiment which has been working well for more than two centuries.

One of our original ideas is *freedom of religion*. Our traditional principle of separation of church and state means that there can be no "established religion" in our land. Yet while no particular religion enjoys a preference, religion itself is favored. Our sessions of Congress begin with a prayer; public officials take office with an oath made to God; our coins proclaim that "in God we trust"; and our courts exist to safeguard religion, not to inhibit it.

Organized religion is strong in our country, with most Americans claiming membership in a formal religious body. Churches and temples of every faith across America are built by the free-will efforts of their people, along with religious institutions of education and charity of every kind. The most recent figures show that 52 percent of U.S. Catholics have shared in the celebration of Mass during the last week.

In the United States there is widespread ecumenical and interfaith cooperation. Your Holiness has often spoken with joy about your meetings in America during 1987 with Protestant and Orthodox officials in Columbia, South Carolina, with Jewish leaders in Miami, and with representatives of non-Christian religions in Los Angeles.

The communications media wield tremendous influence in our country. There is total *freedom of thought* in public educational and cultural media, and any form of censorship is abhorred. While the sources of information are rich indeed, there are often materialistic, secularistic, and hedonistic values widely disseminated among our people in some of our media.

Perhaps most significant of all, the *spirit of democracy* courses through America and influences our lives. Authoritarianism is suspect in any area of learning or culture. Individual freedom is prized supremely. Religious doctrine and moral teaching are widely judged by these criteria. Therefore, to assert that there is a church teaching with authority binding and loosing for eternity is truly a sign of contradiction to many Americans who consider the divine right of bishops as outmoded as the divine right of kings. Accordingly, bishops live and work constantly in this atmosphere.

In these days, Holy Father, we ponder together the challenge of teaching the universal and ageless truth of the Roman Catholic Church in the above-mentioned cultural context of the United States. We value this opportunity. We are here with open minds and open hearts, here to listen and to explain, here to seek wisdom and strength in the presence of the Lord, who has sent us all to preach the good news to all the nations.

The Bishop as Teacher of the Faith

Joseph Cardinal Ratzinger

In the Book of Revelation, it is said of the new city, Jerusalem: "The walls of the city stood on twelve foundation stones, each one of which bore the name of one of the twelve apostles of the Lamb" (21:14). This grand vision of the end-time has to be kept before our eyes in order to understand fully what the Second Vatican Council teaches concerning the office of bishop: "This sacred synod teaches that by divine institution bishops have succeeded to the place of the apostles as shepherds of the church, and he who hears them, hears Christ" (*Lumen Gentium*, 20). It is of the essence of the episcopal office, then, that the bishops "have succeeded to the place of the apostles." The meaning of this is made clear by the fact that they are called "Shepherds of the Church." Reference to the word of Christ sheds further light upon this expression: he who hears you hears me (Lk 10:16). This is important: "the pastoral ministry," the shepherd's office, is explained through the notion of hearing. One is a shepherd according to the mind of Jesus Christ, then, inasmuch as he brings people to the hearing of Christ. In the background here the words of the prologue of John's Gospel calling Christ the *Logos* can be heard; resonant too is the ancient Christian idea that it is precisely the *Logos* who is the Shepherd of men, guiding us sheep who have gone astray to the pastures of truth and giving us there the water of life. To be shepherds, then, means to give voice to the *Logos*, the voice to the redeeming Word.

These basic thoughts come back again in practical form when *Lumen Gentium*, 25, describes in concrete terms what the bishop is to do. The Second Vatican Council stated it in this way: "Among the principal duties of bishops, the preaching of the Gospel occupies an eminent place," which, incidentally, is the repetition of a formula coined by the Council of Trent (Session 24, *De Reform.* IV, eds. Alberigo et al., Bologna 1973, p. 763). First and foremost, the

13

bishop is an evangelist; and we might put it this way: it is as an evangelist that he is a successor of the apostles.

If we as bishops examine our consciences upon the words of that sentence and ask ourselves whether our actual priorities correspond to this ideal, there are within the developments of this post-conciliar era certainly many positive elements according with this image of the bishop which one could adduce: In general, bishops do actually preach more today than was formerly the case—perhaps sometimes too much. It is surely a positive development that bishops themselves almost always preach at pontifical functions and thus take precedence over their priests in proclaiming the Word of God. Along the same line, we find intensified efforts on the part of many bishops and bishops' conferences to comment by means of well-prepared pastoral letters upon the great issues of the day and to respond to them in the light of the faith. The balance is seen to tip much less toward the positive, however, as soon as we begin to think about the developments in catechesis in the post-conciliar period. To a large extent, this area has been turned over to the so-called professional. This, in turn, has led to an excess of experimentation, which often makes the actual topic vanish from sight, and to a confusion of voices, making it all the more difficult to recognize that of the Gospel. The problem becomes more evident if we think about the relationship between bishop and theologians who are no longer active in just the quiet realm of academic research and teaching. They frequently perform their quite dissonant concert for all the public with the instruments of the mass media in such a way that their voice drowns out that of the bishop-evangelist. Despite all the indisputable efforts by bishops to proclaim the Word, theologians in many parts of the world have taken the place of the bishop as teacher. Although much good has also come to pass in this way, on the whole the result has to be seen predominantly as one of uncertainty and confusion: the contours of the faith are vanishing behind reflections which ought to be illuminating it.

In this context, I have to mention a particular development of this post-conciliar time which calls for our special attention. We heard how the Second Vatican Council gave precedence to the bishop's mission of proclaiming the Word. If we would look now at the theological literature of the period after the Council on this question, we would discover surprisingly that this statement has remained practically without commentary. What we find instead in the literature are explanations which attempt to reduce the episcopate to a kind of spiritual administration. Thus, J. Colson asserted an equivalence between the early Christian bishop and the *mebaqqer* of the Qumran Community, and he strove to verify that this was the model James and the other early Christian leaders followed. After the manner of Qumran, they were only "supervisors." The patrologist, A. Hamman, takes a similar position regarding the Greek world: The bishops were called *episkopoi*, which means "inspectors" according to the linguistic usage current in the civil administration of that time. Hans Küng establishes the same etymological and genealogical point and from it draws his distinction between bishops and teachers, his separation of teaching from the function of shepherds. All these theses have not remained in the academic realm; rather they have been transformed into a kind of pressure which is exerted upon the bishop: it would be his task to avoid polarizations, to appear as a moderator acting within the plurality of existing opinions; but he himself is not to become "partisan" in any substantive way. Now this is always correct, if the question is just one of scholarly differences. But it is wrong, if what comes into issue is the faith itself. For the faith, entry into the Church does not constitute a "partisan act."

Actually, we have to confess that bishops have submitted in large measure to this scheme of things and have little exercised their teaching authority in opposition to theologians. This course, however, has at the same time caused their own preaching activity to depreciate because the preached word is consigned to the category of the simply "pastoral" and is not invested with the authority of decision. But this is precisely when it is not pastoral, for pastoral activity consists in placing man at the point of decision, confronting him with the authority of the truth. What is preached conforms to the norm of the psalmist's words: "You have made known to me the path of life" (Ps 16:11).

The German philosopher, Robert Spaemann, made a sarcastic comment upon this psalm verse some time ago: "To dally long in a Catholic bookstore does not encourage one to pray with the psalmist: 'You have made known to me the path to life.' There we have learned that in no way did Jesus change water into wine; insights into the art have actually succeeded instead in changing wine into water! This new brand of magic bears the name *aggiornamento*."

In making our examination of conscience, the question now arises: Why to so large an extent have we bishops acquiesced in

15

this reduction of our office to the inspector, the moderator, the *mebaqqer*? Why have we gone back to Qumran when it comes to this essential point of the New Testament? This is where we encounter the background of our modern culture, the issue of the proper relationship between this culture and the Gospel. Modern culture tells us first of all that it is not possible to distinguish clearly between faith and theology and, even if it should be possible, it can only be the specialist in any case, the theologian not the shepherd, who is competent. How should the shepherd be able to find his way in such a thicket? The shepherd, then, cannot determine whether theological reflection has begun perhaps to erode the faith itself and has forfeited his role of service.

This is just the first stage of the problem. The real question is more radical. Our modern world makes a distinction between two spheres of life, that of action and that of reflection. In the sphere of action, a person needs something like authority which is functionally based and which becomes active within the framework of its area of operation. In the sphere of reflection, there can be no authority. Reflection follows solely the laws of thought. Its essence, however, is such that it recognizes no final validity to its process, just the ever new hypothesis, which must be tested and which, at given times, has to be overhauled. What this means, though, is this: The Church can exercise a functional authority within the sphere of her dealings, for authority is based upon functional contexts, nothing else. The Church cannot interfere in the course of thought, in the scientific reflection of theology. Theology is not a matter of authority, but rather one of being professional. These notions have attained such a degree of plausibility in the world of today that it is well nigh impossible for bishops not to succumb to them. However, if these notions hold sway, this means that the Church, while surely able to dispense pious advice, will not be able to bear witness to the truth in a way that is binding and, thereby, to call people to a commitment.

Involved with this, there is a final problem: In the hierarchy of values of today's world, the free rights of the individual and those accorded to the mass media take highest place while the objective moral values, about which there is no agreement anyway, are banished to the realm of the individual, where they merit no public defense from the community. There is, to put it bluntly, a right to act immorally, but morality itself has no rights. In contrast to the one-sidedness of former epochs, this can have its advantage. On

16

the other hand, the commission of witnessing to the truth of the Gospel brings one also to suffering for it.

But this is at the same time the very positive conclusion toward which our deliberations have been leading: It is the hallmark of truth to be worth suffering for. In the deepest sense of the word, the evangelist must also be a martyr. If he is unwilling to be so, he should not lay his hand to the plow. It goes without saying that the bishop, as messenger of the Gospel, has to be generous in giving space for intellectual disputation. He has to be ready to learn himself and to accept correction. But he must also realize that the faith, which is expressed in the baptismal symbol and which he has inherited from the witnesses of all the centuries preceding, calls him to a responsibility. The word with which Paul bade farewell to the presbyters in Ephesus touches us too: "Keep watch over yourselves and over the whole flock over which the Holy Spirit has appointed you as bishops that you might care for it as Shepherds of God's Church which he acquired for himself through the Blood of his Son. . . . Be on guard therefore" (Acts 20:28,31).

John Cardinal O'Connor

When it was published that I was to present this paper, certain people asked whom I *know*, to be given this honor. As I tried to prepare the paper, I found myself asking: Who doesn't *like* me, that I should be given this task?

The topic assigned is "The Bishop as Teacher of the Faith" within the context of the culture and society of the United States.

Permit me to make a major departure immediately. I cannot imagine that *any* bishop is unaware of his teaching role as explicated in tradition, conciliar documents, canon law, and the example of our Holy Father. If I am to add anything useful, then, to Cardinal Ratzinger's eloquent remarks, I believe it will be only by way of suggesting some of the problems bishops encounter in the United States in trying conscientiously to carry out their teaching role.

First, however, let me make clear that the bishops of the United States have been first and foremost articulate and courageous teachers of the faith for the two centuries of our existence. I make this point because U.S. bishops are too often patronizingly dismissed as mere builders, administrators, and fund-raisers. Some church historians and theologians clearly consider U.S. bishops hopelessly illiterate.

The fact is that American bishops have been teaching for two centuries by way of their homilies, pastoral letters, liturgies, confirmation ceremonies, diocesan newspapers. They teach by their works, their institutions for the sick and the aged, their maintenance of the highest standards of medical ethics in their hospitals, their care for the homeless and the hungry, and so on. Many holy bishops teach the primacy of the spiritual by their very lives. American bishops are preeminently teachers. I believe that the teaching commitment *and* effectiveness of the U.S. bishops is comparable to that of any body of bishops in the world.

But there are serious impediments to the teaching *effectiveness* of American bishops. Some impediments, I suspect, are common to the world at large. Others that we tend to see as peculiarly American are also fairly common elsewhere. Still others are unique to the United States.

18

Universal Impediments to Episcopal Teaching

Two impediments to effective episcopal teaching which I suspect are relatively common to the episcopacy throughout the world relate, respectively, to Vatican II and *Humanae Vitae*, though caused by neither.

First, Vatican II. While there was a reasonable amount of preparation by various commissions *prior* to the deliberations of Vatican II, there was virtually no post-Vatican II preparation of the Church at large to receive, understand, and rationally implement the conciliar documents. We are still trying to recover from the chaos of misunderstanding and deliberate distortions. A tremendous number of American Catholics, at least, learned all they thought they had to know about the Council from the mysterious and ubiquitous Xavier Rynne of the *New Yorker* magazine. This is terribly serious. We still have millions of Catholics, and not a few priests and religious, who talk esoterically about the "spirit" of Vatican II—accusing many bishops of resisting that spirit—when they themselves have never read a single council document. I had to spend four years in New York in preparation for a synod in getting people to study the conciliar documents. Because of this gross ignorance, many people, equating abstinence from fish on Friday with the validity of the Holy Trinity, gave up the latter—and much other church teaching—when they learned they were no longer bound by the former.

Suddenly all the old certainties seemed to be in question. Many Catholics felt betrayed. They felt the rug had been pulled out from under their most sacred and certain beliefs. Well-intended liturgical experiments permitted to run wild naturalized the supernatural even more, desacralized the sacred for large numbers of young people. (*Lex orandi est lex credendi.*) Even worse, the vacuum in understanding of the faith left by failure to prepare the people for the documents of the Council was too often filled by false prophets with false interpretations of the Council and particularly with ambiguous ecclesiologies. If *nature* abhors a vacuum, the publishing industry simply won't even *permit* a vacuum.

The second major impediment to episcopal teaching throughout the world, I believe, developed out of the manner of preparing for, the extensive delay in the promulgation of, and the variety of interpretations given to *Humanae Vitae*. I believe that circumstances surrounding the publication of *Humanae Vitae* seriously eroded the credibility of church teaching. I am not for a moment questioning the validity of *Humanae Vitae*. I am saying that when Catholics learned—and it took them no time at all—that they could shop around among confessors for opinions on birth control, they soon decided that they really didn't have to confess the matter at all. In my judgment, we have not yet recovered from this confusion. One gets a sense that a kind of moral free enterprise system took over at some point. The "moral market" has been allowed to float.

These two general impediments to episcopal teaching have affected the Church, I repeat, almost universally and certainly the Church in the United States. Let me turn, now, first to some familiar problems for episcopal teaching in America (and elsewhere), then to some cultural problems rather unique to America, but often unnoticed.

"American" Impediments

A. Commonly Recognized Problems (Not Unique to America)

Bishops must teach largely through others: priests, religious, deacons, lay persons. While it is unfortunate that not all of our priests preach effectively, this problem is reasonably correctable. Harder to correct, however, is the loss of teaching religious and the theological or ecclesiological confusion demonstrated by some—by no means all—who still do teach. Teachers committed to radical feminism, for example, whether priests, religious, or lay, are quite capable of distorting doctrine. At the same time, it must be admitted that sexism is a reality. It provides grist for the mill of radical feminism and threatens the credibility of bishops who try to teach about justice—as does serious underpayment of lay persons, men and women, who work for the Church. Most troublesome of all "isms," however, is racism, which makes a mockery of episcopal teaching about the sacredness of every human person. That it still plagues the Church is tragically obvious.

The media and the movies are often horrifying perverters of family values and constitute very grave obstacles to episcopal teaching. (See, for example, William Lynch, SJ, *The Image Industries: A Constructive Analysis of Films and Television*, Sheed and Ward, New York, 1959. ". . .[W]e are dealing with a question of the largest national movement when we talk of the present and future state of the mass media among us. . . . Those who wish to live with the ostriches and to deny this fact are free to do so, but whatever history lies ahead of us will put them down as children for their denial," pp. 157-158.) A view that Catholicism has canonized capitalism is a severe obstacle to teaching social and economic justice in some quarters. (Some Catholics have learned too well Max Weber's *The Protestant Ethic and the Spirit of Capitalism*.) Both "rightist" and "leftist" newspapers and journals that call themselves Catholic but constantly attack bishops, individually and collectively, are surely an impediment to the teaching ministry. In a world of constant flux, it is difficult for bishops to be heard when they teach that the Church still exists primarily to help people reach an eternal goal.

Continuing the list almost at random, honesty compels me to suggest that Rome can contribute to confusion if it releases papal or other documents to the press before the bishops receive them. The press publishes selectively as it will. The bishop, supposedly the authority, is put in the position of reacting without having seen a document. Another problem of note: ambiguity about the authority of local ordinaries relative to local Catholic colleges and universities may permit distortions of church teaching to go unchallenged. At the same time, the peculiarities of the American church-state system and legitimate questions concerning funding, academic freedom, and other knotty issues generate complex problems for Catholic college and university presidents who want to serve the Church faithfully.

Poor selection, training, or supervision of campus ministers can result in seriously depriving Catholic college students of orthodox guidance. Years of confusion and diversity in catechetical instructional materials used in both Catholic schools and in catechetical programs outside Catholic schools have left an entire generation in a state of ambiguity. Some bishops seem to have been virtually bludgeoned into compliance by some of the publishing companies that have produced misleading religious education materials; others seem to have been browbeaten by directors of religious education or teachers of religion, whom they perceive to be much more authoritative than themselves. Episcopal feelings of inadequacy are heightened when bishops are told patronizingly, or even contemptuously, that new teaching *methods* must determine teaching *content*.

This brings up what I believe to be critical: that a certain number of bishops at some point during the past 20 years or so have seemed to lose confidence, first in themselves as persons, then in their magisterial authority, perhaps in the face of some hard-hitting theologians, perhaps out of fear of the press. (*Mirabile dictu!*) At times the bishop convinces himself that peace is the highest good. Sometimes, if I may say so respectfully, a bishop may not want to enter battle over authoritative church teaching called into doubt by dissenting theologians, pastors, religious, lay persons, or the secular or religious press because he fears that neither the National Conference of Catholic Bishops nor Rome will support him. He may consider twisting slowly in the wind to be highly unepiscopal and inordinately uncomfortable.

Time permits but a few other problems in this category of "commonly recognized problems." For example, we are blessed in the United States today with many millions of immigrants. Few, however, bring their own priests. We are all short of priests after years of failure to attract vocations and the teaching by some that God is telling us this is the day of lay persons, so that priests aren't terribly important. We are particularly short of priests who are linguistically and culturally equipped to teach these newcomers. The potential losses to the faith are grave, especially losses to Pentecostal sects. Another problem: We are justifiably proud of our Catholic schools, but the costs are escalating every day and bordering on the impossible. The threat to our Catholic schools, unsubsidized in our country by the government, may be one of the gravest teaching obstacles our bishops will have to face for generations.

Still another problem in this same general category: While we have so many outstanding Catholics, we do have those for whom their political party is virtually their religion. No matter what the political party's platform or what the moral positions of its candidates, their party loyalty, often inherited generation by generation, makes it difficult for them to vote as an informed conscience and an understanding of Catholic teaching would suggest. This is a realistic aspect of the American political system and must be understood, however difficult it is for teaching bishops.

Next, we are developing in our country with frightening speed a consistent ethic of death, with some 20 million abortions since

1973, and euthanasia under a variety of euphemistic terms becoming acceptable to the point that laws authorizing outright suicide may be just around the corner.

Finally, within this category of "commonly recognized problems" (and this could require a paper of its own), we are still recovering from Vietnam. In a letter of April 23, 1866, Karl Marx wrote to Friedrich Engels, "After the Civil War phase the United States are really only now entering the revolutionary phase. . . ." Nothing since the Civil War has so torn our country and induced revolution as our involvement in Vietnam. With millions of young people, every form of the Establishment lost credibility: government, business, education, the family, the Church. In the general climate of disenchantment, traditional values were rejected as having been responsible for the war. "Free love" became widespread, as did drugs. Authority—all authority—became suspect, then rejected by many. I suspect that only an American can appreciate fully the impact of this war on the teaching mission and credibility of U.S. bishops.

B. Underlying Problems Less Commonly Recognized (Unique to America)

Now to my second category of problems, which are uniquely American and uniquely cultural, but which I believe affect us largely at the unconscious level, or that at least often escape notice and identification. A culture, after all, is rarely, if ever, either deliberately designed as such or learned as such. While formal study can help us *analyze* a culture, we usually learn a culture— become enculturated—by osmosis. Culture is the confluence of many forces and variables.

I suggest that a number of these uniquely American cultural problems, impediments to episcopal teaching, are born of the peculiar political, moral, psychological, and philosophical culture of our country. They help make up the American experience. Bear with me, please, then, on what may seem an exotic, if not indeed a pedantic journey. My purpose is exceedingly practical. I believe that both the Holy See and the bishops of the United States can better appreciate why it is difficult to teach the faith in all its purity in the United States, if both understand especially the three intertwined cultural forces set forth below, however simplistically because of the press of time. These cultural forces are (1) the moral

philosophies that are at the heart of the American experience;
(2) group dynamics and process; (3) pluralism.

1. Moral Philosophies and the American Experience

Bishops in the United States have always had to teach within a cultural context of four different moral philosophies, three of them uncongenial to church teaching, namely, pragmatism, utilitarianism, social evolutionism. The fourth, natural moral law, is of course quite congenial to church teaching. (William H. Marnell describes these philosophies in his *Man-made Morals: Four Philosophies that Shaped America*, Doubleday and Co., New York, 1966.)

However many of the Founding Fathers were deists or pure rationalists, they were grounded in natural moral law, even though modified for them by John Locke. They grasped its premises and used them to shape the Declaration of Independence and at least the Bill of Rights of the Constitution. Catholicism is preeminently attuned to the basic principles of the American republic as articulated by the Founding Fathers in large measure because of Catholicism's affinity with *natural moral law*. I suggest that Catholic moral teaching has been accepted or rejected in our country in almost direct proportion to the acceptance or rejection of natural moral law in the formulation of public policy. Debates over critical moral issues have inevitably reflected this: slavery, racism, abortion, euthanasia, homosexuality, and war are illustrative.

Justice Oliver Wendell Holmes, Jr., was the most famous Supreme Court justice our country has ever known, the justice most commonly cited in law schools ever since his day, and the author of the classic text, *The Common Law*. Justice Holmes explicitly rejected all appeal to natural moral law in interpreting the Constitution. In its place, he substituted the philosophy of *pragmatism*: the good is whatever works or is expedient. Moral relativism entered jurisprudence and American life by way of pragmatism, which is unconditionally hostile to all moral absolutes. I suggest that, simultaneously, the law has become the primary teacher in America. Whatever is legal is assumed to be morally good. Abortion and homosexuality, for example, are legal, hence assumed to be moral. The horrifying rise in court-assisted "euthanasia" I believe to be ultimately traceable to Justice Holmes and to his medical doctor father.

Jeremy Bentham's *utilitarianism* took American form by way of the "greatest happiness of the greatest number," a rationale which takes advantage of a political philosophy that the majority rules. It is an easy step to the concept that majority rule determines what is morally good for everyone. Again the thrust is to reject moral absolutes or teaching about intrinsic good and evil. Doctrine becomes irrelevant.

Not the philosophical founder, but certainly the most powerful proponent of *social Darwinism* or *social evolutionism* was President Theodore Roosevelt, with his hearty but destructive emphasis on "rugged individualism." The "survival of the fittest" became the canon of all social morality. I suggest that whenever America has been imperialistic, as in its early 20th-century attitude toward Filipinos, or carried away by its self-perceived "manifest destiny," the philosophy of social evolution has been the driving and destructive force. No American philosophy has been more antagonistic to the social gospel taught by American bishops. Worse, none has been more antagonistic to the belief that all men are created equal or to our belief in the worth, the dignity, the sacredness of every human person as made in the image of God. Much of today's homelessness, bad housing, inadequate concern for the poor of the world, and especially a subtle contempt for the Third World, is rooted in this moral philosophy. *Redemptor Hominis*, with its emphasis on man as "the way," wouldn't stand a chance under rugged individualism and the survival of the fittest, even if Andrew Carnegie built a financial empire on the backs of the unrugged and the unsurvivable. Friedrich Nietzsche's *Ubermensch*, on the contrary, would fit in very well. (Many familiar names can be found among the shapers of relativistic moral philosophies for America: Charles Darwin, Thomas Huxley, Herbert Spencer, William Graham Sumner, Justice Stephen J. Field, et al.)

2. Group Dynamics and Process

The Vienna Circle, particularly Wittgenstein and Schlick, reached out to America by the way of the Cambridge school of analysis. Logical positivism did not have to attack metaphysics. It simply treated metaphysical propositions as meaningless. Only the observable, the measurable, became important. American psychology became, through John Watson, the mere study of observable—therefore external—behavior. John Dewey turned the psychology of *behaviorism* into an educational philosophy of *instrumentalism*, which in large part, by way of Columbia Teachers College in New York, came to influence hundreds of thousands of teachers across America, including religious, and a very great number of educational institutions throughout the United States. In essence, learning was to be measured by change in external behavior; the purpose of teaching was to effect such change.

In the meanwhile, the force of Julien Lamettrie's *L'Homme Machine* was at work in Norbert Wiener's research in cybernetics or feedback mechanisms, and another physicist, Kurt Lewin, was busily developing group dynamics, the social application of such exotic mathematical concepts as topology and hodology. Relationships between peoples were determined by vectors and valences. In time, Lewin's disciples were devising theories about *lifespace*. Bethel, Maine, became the summer teaching center for schoolteachers, again including religious, who wanted to learn about sociodrama. Encounter groups and sensitivity sessions deluged the country very soon thereafter, and America was caught up in dialogue, which was frequently unrelated to the exchange of information or the communication of truths. Dialogue was simply a process intended to achieve consensus. Dialogue was successful or unsuccessful only to the degree in which consensus occurred or failed to occur. Substance became irrelevant. The medium became the message.

I suggest that this entire development, rooted in the Vienna Circle, in which metaphysical propositions were considered meaningless, played a major role in the emergence of consensus theology, in which ontological truth plays little role. I suggest further that as seminaries stopped teaching philosophy, and particularly metaphysics, theology lost the language of substance and of absolutes. Theological speculation became a search for consensus, which in turn was found in *praxis*, the theological equivalent of *process*. Popular, observable behavior became the norm of truth. The formation of conscience became almost a lost art, as did the practice of confession for huge numbers, since the entire notion of *sin* became at best speculative. I suggest that an unnoticed result of group dynamics and process which has made episcopal teaching exceedingly difficult is a form of anti-intellectualism. The true and the good can be discerned only by *feeling*. It was understandable that many young people turned to Zen, while others turned to hard rock music, drugs, and free-for-all sex. (It is nostalgic to read Fulton J. Sheen's *Preface to Religion*, written in 1946 [P. J. Kennedy and Sons, New York]: "An unequivocal voice in your moral consciousness that your acts of wrongdoing are abnormal facts in your nature" [p. 35]. *Utinam!* St. Paul's Epistle to the Romans might describe reality much better today for millions. Until a new and serious recovery of commitment to "forming consciences" and young people are again taught about the confessional, moral insensitivity rooted in moral ignorance will be a major impediment to episcopal teaching.)

3. Pluralism

Every American bishop, including myself, would fight fiercely to preserve the American pluralistic political system, safeguarded in part by constitutional checks and balances and by a very strong commitment to the principle of "one person, one vote." I do not know a single American bishop who would opt for a state church. It has taken 200 years and some serious mistakes to get our system to work, and it's still far from perfect. There can be no serious question, however, but that the Church has profited in countless ways.

Political pluralism has been undergoing changes, however, in a direction feared by some of the Founding Fathers, leaning toward the "tyranny of the minority." Combined with the politically valid principle of "one person, one vote," political pluralism, particularly in this deviant form of the tyranny of the minority, offers an alluring rationalization for a unique and pervasive form of theology of dissent. Magisterial teaching becomes no more authoritative than the opinion of any single individual, as my vote is as good as yours. The response to a magisterium that attempts to "impose" church teaching is to organize into a vociferous minority, co-opt the media and charge the magisterium—or even the Holy Father—with the most heinous of crimes in the American lexicon: *discrimination*. This has been one of the most powerful weapons in the arsenal of radical feminism, for example, used with equal zeal by some theologians who have championed that cause.

27

Pope Paul VI recognized "pluralism of research and thought, which explores and expounds dogma in different ways, but without eliminating its objective meaning . . . as a natural component of catholicity, and a sign of cultural riches and of personal commitment on the part of those who belong together. . . ." The same pope admitted that "a balanced theological pluralism finds its foundation in the very mystery of Christ, the unfathomable riches of which go beyond the capacities of expression of all ages and all cultures. . . ." He observed further: "The doctrine of the faith . . . calls for ever new investigations . . . the perspectives of the Word of God are so numerous, and the perspectives of the faithful who study it are so numerous, that convergence in the same faith is never exempt from personal particularities in the adherence of each one. However . . . the magisterium of the Church . . . as the proximate norm, determines the faith of all and, at the same time, guarantees everyone against the subjective judgment of all divergent interpretations of the faith."

So far, so good, but Pope Paul VI speaks quite differently of the notion of pluralism that I believe to be, in our own country, an illicit extension of political pluralism.

What are we to say of a pluralism that considers faith and its expression not as a common and therefore ecclesial heritage but as *an individual rediscovery* of free criticism and free examination of God's word? In fact, without the mediation of the Magisterium of the Church to which the Apostles entrusted their own magisterium and which, consequently, teaches only "what was transmitted," secure union with Christ through the Apostles, namely, "those who transmit what they have themselves received," is compromised. For this reason, once perseverance in doctrine transmitted by the Apostles is compromised, it happens that, wishing perhaps to elude the difficulties of the mystery, formulas of illusory comprehensibility are sought which dissolve its real content; in this way *doctrines are constructed which do not adhere to the objectivity of the faith* or which are even contrary to it, and furthermore contain elements that contradict one another. . . . The process we have described (the obscuring of the role of the Church) takes the form of a doctrinal dissent which claims to be sponsored by theological pluralism and which is not infrequently carried to the point of dogmatic relativism. . . . The internal oppositions affecting the different sectors of ecclesial life, if they are stabilized in a state of dissent, lead to setting up against the one institution and community of salvation, a plurality of institutions or communities of dissent which are not in conformity with the nature of the Church.

(Hence, the bedeviling question of a variety of ecclesiologies.)

Pope John Paul II summarizes it all in *Redemptor Hominis*:

> In the field of human knowledge, which is continually being broadened and yet differentiated, faith too must be investigated deeply, manifesting the magnitude of revealed mystery and attending toward an understanding of truth, which has in God its one supreme source. If it is permissible and even desirable that the enormous work to be done in this direction should take into consideration a certain pluralism of methodology, the work cannot however depart from the fundamental unity of the teaching of faith and morals which is that work's end. Accordingly, close collaboration by theology with the magisterium is indispensable. Every theologian must be particularly aware of what Christ Himself stated when He said: *"The word which you hear is not mine but the Father's who sent me."* Nobody, therefore, can make of theology as it were a simple collection of his own personal ideas, but everybody must be aware of being in close union with the mission of teaching truth for which the Church is responsible.

While for the sake of clarity I have proposed these three types of uniquely "American" cultural forces confronting bishops in our culture in separate categories, they are obviously not discrete from one another. On the contrary, they spill over into one another and reinforce one another, as the swirling together of many different bodies of water in which American bishops must swim while trying to help God's people reach solid ground—the rock of the Church. If American bishops occasionally feel they are drowning, or gasping for breath, the experience is eminently understandable.

In my view, it is to the credit of American bishops, individually and collectively, that they have succeeded so frequently and so well in keeping God's people afloat. One hears it said, at times, that the Holy See does not understand the United States; hence, that the Holy See does not appreciate the faith, the integrity, and the loyalty of the bishops of the United States. Be that as it may, in my judgment, it would be helpful for the Holy See to recognize that frequently when American bishops are perceived as questioning the authority of the Holy See, what they are really doing is trying to make things "work" in our culture—that is, to apply and to integrate into our culture in a meaningful and enduring way those Catholic teachings to which the culture is at least alien, if not hostile. This, respectfully, is what I believe the Holy See must understand if indeed misunderstanding has in fact occurred. At the same time, it goes without elucidating that the American bishops must always recognize the Holy See's responsibility to preserve the catholicity of our faith and must take the long view of the Church in all lands and all ages. To discredit either the Holy See or the American bishops because of the problems confronting both is to discredit Noah's ark because of the flood.

I believe I see a new phenomenon developing in the United States, which, again, it would be mutually helpful for both Rome and the U.S. bishops to understand. Through innumerable court decisions that have made moral relativism the norm, the inordinate power of television and movies that glorify sex and violence, and are inimical to family values and cynical of all authority, a public educational system that has been almost totally secularized, and various other factors, our American culture has been changing dramatically in recent years. In response, I see the Church more and more becoming a counterculture, a voice crying in the wilderness. One need but examine recent documents of the National Conference of Catholic Bishops to discover this trend. In my judgment, it is a trend that must continue. The great preacher-teacher Archbishop Fulton J. Sheen said it very clearly: "What the world needs is a voice that is right, not when the world is right, but a voice that is right when the world is wrong."

Finally, I am not unaware that those who assigned me to prepare this paper really didn't ask me to append my personal advice, but I must run the risk. First, I believe it could help both Rome and U.S. bishops if we would declare a moratorium on the use of the terms *liberal* and *conservative*. These are political terms unworthy of bishops as teachers. Paul VI reminded us that orthodoxy is the Church's main concern, and the pastoral office is her most important, divinely willed mission. Orthodoxy is neither liberal nor conservative, right wing or left wing. Orthodoxy is orthodoxy, and we're all committed to it, lock, stock, and barrel, however differently we may express ourselves as individuals.

Second, I would suggest that while every bishop must teach with unambiguous clarity and courage—the courage of an Ignatius in the jaws of the lions—we must keep both our balance and our sense of humor. Nietzsche said, "The world no longer believes because believers no longer sing." St. Augustine gave us the song: "You are an Easter people, and your song is Alleluia!" Pope John XXIII warned us not to be prophets of doom. God is not finished with us yet. The resurrection is not yet complete, the Body of Christ not yet fully built up.

Third, there is an awful lot of good in our American culture, and we bishops have learned from America even while teaching it. And we have learned to live with its evils while not being deceived by them. Our Holy Father has seen for himself the magnificent faith of countless millions of our people. Some are weak, as we their bishops are weak; some are sinful, as we their bishops are sinful; all are very human, as are we their bishops. St. Augustine succeeded in baptizing Plato, rather than accepting his paganism. St. Thomas succeeded in baptizing Aristotle, rather than succumbing to his naturalistic philosophy. If thus far we bishops may seem to have accommodated too comfortably to the moral relativism that characterizes much of American life, give us time. We have lots of water in our country, and we'll baptize our culture yet. Some of us may not be outstanding theologians, but when the chips are down, as we say in America, we know who we are. We subscribe completely to Vatican II's *Verbum Dei*, that our preaching is ". . . the preaching of those who have received through episcopal succession the sure gift of truth" (no. 8).

The Priests, Agents of Evangelization

Antonio Cardinal Innocenti

In my presentation, after recognizing the great contribution and service offered by American priests, I hope to offer some suggestions for the renewal and revival of priestly life and ministry in the Church in the United States.

These observations are based on information and reports which have reached the Congregation, including the very helpful up-to-date information provided by the quinquennial reports and the meetings with the various groups of bishops during their *Ad Limina* visits last year. Because of time limitations, it will be necessary to proceed *per summa capita* leaving the development of the various issues which are raised to the discussion period.

I.

1. Positive Developments

As a whole, the clergy of the United States show many positive and encouraging qualities, which are all the more commendable because they are displayed in a historical and sociocultural context which is sometimes indifferent, or even hostile, to them.

I would like to single out the commitment of priests to the renewal called for by the Second Vatican Council in the liturgy and in pastoral ministry, as well as their participation in the new structures created to encourage fraternity and coresponsibility, such as the council of priests and programs of continuing education. In addition, they have made efforts to involve the laity in the life of the Church. Their ministry is characterized by a reaching out in charity to the needy, by a missionary and ecumenical spirit, by a concern for the alienated, and by a remarkable sensitivity to social problems.

We cannot overlook their strong commitment to pastoral care, which is always accompanied by a search for new approaches and models, and by an increasing attention to the Hispanic immigrants and other minorities. The bishops openly recognize these positive qualities, which inspire hope for the future.

2. Problematic Aspects

In addition to these positive aspects, there are others which are problematic and somewhat negative. It is only right to consider these problems in the hope of finding solutions for them.

Objectively speaking, there is a certain amount of anxiety and unrest among a good number of priests in the United States. Various studies point to a wide variety of causes for the present state of affairs: deficient formation in the seminaries; loss of the priest's prestige in society and the consequent lack of understanding of his priestly mission; and the disorientation or lack of security provoked by conflicting ecclesiological models in the United States.

To overcome these difficulties, priests need powerful supernatural motivation, which will fortify and sustain them and help them resist all those threats to their vocation and priestly identity which are found either *intra ecclesiam* or in American society. This motivation will be possible only if three conditions are met:

a) Stricter and more demanding criteria should be applied in the identification of an authentic priestly vocation.

b) In formation programs both before and after ordination, priests need more solid preparation in philosophy, theology, and the spiritual/ascetical life.

c) Priests need a specific kind of spirituality inspired by the principle *nolite conformari huic saeculo.* Only in this way will they be immune to the temptations of modern society and be able more closely and freely to imitate Christ, the Good Shepherd.

This must be the bishop's point of departure in his primary responsibility as the father and head of the diocesan presbyterate. As father and head, he is also responsible for the education of his priests and for the preservation of their priestly identity. Among the practical pastoral suggestions which the Congregation would like to offer the bishops to help them meet this important responsibility, I would like to emphasize the following three:

1. *The bishop must be close to his priests.* He should have frequent contact with them and be willing to open himself up to them, particularly on such occasions as the meetings of the priests' council or of the continuing education program or during retreats, days of recollection, and periodic visits to the parishes.

2. *The bishops must make the constant effort to create and reinforce the priest's sense of belonging to a common presbyterate.* He should strengthen the bonds of fraternity among the priests, who are called, with him and under him, to be a sign of the charity of Christ as this is expressed in the priestly life.

3. *The bishop should provide an ongoing "education" for his priests* to make them more keenly aware of their calling to serve the people of their society *in persona Christi* and to transform this society through the Word and sacraments, of which they must be credible witnesses.

II.

Using as our point of departure the strategical principles just outlined, we will attempt to delineate the essential characteristics of the priest as a key figure in the evangelization of North American society.

a) *The proclamation of the Word of God* is the first task of the priest, who must be conscious of the fact that, in virtue of his priestly ministry, which distinguishes him from all the other baptized, he proclaims the Word with the authority conferred by Christ on his apostles and on their successors. Such a mission requires a special honesty and fidelity of the priest to the Word of God, as it is mediated by the magisterium of the Roman pontiff and of the bishops in communion with him. Accordingly, in the exercise of his specific ministry, the priest must pray, study, and be careful so that he avoids the temptation of preaching himself, his own subjective interpretations, or the doctrines of the various ideologies. This is particularly true with respect to Catholic moral doctrine which is presented in homilies, catechesis, and in the ministry of reconciliation. As for the bishops, they must guarantee that their priests, especially those who teach in seminaries and in Catholic schools or who are involved with the mass media, present the doctrines of the Church to the faithful without distortions or erroneous subjective interpretations.

b) *In the pastoral activity of priests, catechesis must occupy a privileged place* because, by reason of his vocation and mission, the priest is the catechist of the community. This is a responsibility inherent in his priestly identity which he cannot delegate to anyone else. However, it happens here or there that priests delegate this task to lay people and remain partially or totally uninvolved in the catechetical ministry. The involvement of the laity in this area is desirable and is encouraged by the Church, but this does not exempt the priest from taking personal responsibility for both the formation and guidance of the lay catechists and the orthodoxy and integrity of what is taught as the Catholic faith.

In a time which is characterized by a crisis of the Catholic schools and of religious instruction, by the failure of families to participate in the religious formation of the young, and by the totalitarian influence of the mass media, which impose a vision of life which is, to say the least, areligious, the priest must sense the urgency of his mission and must be able to respond to the emergency situations of modern life with emergency solutions, engaging as many co-workers as possible and exploiting every possible occasion for catechesis in full communion with the bishop.

c) *The celebration of the Eucharist and of the sacrament of reconciliation* confer on the priest the *res* and *ratio* of his specific identity among the people of God, since it is mostly in these two sacraments that his acting *in persona Christi* becomes evident. In the present atmosphere of desacralization, it is necessary to stress the uniqueness and indispensability of this person who has been transformed in the depths of his being by the sacrament of holy orders. It is not a question of claiming a social or privileged status for the priest, but of reasserting the Catholic teaching on the priesthood of Christ, in which ordained ministers participate in a unique and irreplaceable way.

In this context, it is fitting to call attention to *the problem of the shortage of priests* and to the various attempts or proposals to resolve the problem which obfuscate or adulterate the truth and reality of the Catholic priesthood. Under the pressure of having to provide pastoral care for communities without enough priests, the Church's pastors appeal to the collaboration of lay people and entrust them with tasks and functions which belong properly to the priest. In this way, *sensim sine sensu*, a leveling of the distinction between priest and laity takes place in the mind of the faithful, which will have serious consequences in the future. For this reason the Congregation for the Clergy urges the pastors of the dioceses not to imagine that the priest shortage can be resolved by aprogressive "clericalization" of the laity who exercise the so-called lay ministries. The only true solution is a farsighted and courageous commitment to priestly vocations and to a defense of the priestly identity as we know it from Scripture and tradition.

d) The evangelization of a modern society like that of the United States needs more than ever *trustworthy and solid witnesses to spiritual and religious ideals*. For this reason, the priest is called to be, and must be formed to be, a man of prayer. The Church entrusts the priest in a special way with liturgical prayer. This means, above all, the Eucharist and the Liturgy of the Hours, as well as the personal prayer which is rooted in a specifically priestly spirituality. It is not easy today for priests to live this dimension of prayer, meditation, and interior silence, caught up as they are in a whirlwind of tasks, relationships, contacts, meetings and immersed in a society where the sound and the image are all-important.

Nevertheless, the fruitfulness of the priest's ministry depends on his commitment to prayer and to the kind of life which privileges reflection and interiority. It is essential, therefore, to resist the tendency to turn the priest into a "manager," rather than a man of prayer. The priest must give top priority to the life of adoration, to the ministry of reconciliation, and to the spiritual direction of souls. He must dedicate himself to caring for the sick, visiting families, and reaching out to young people. Only if he is committed to this kind of life will a true evangelization take place.

III.

I would like to conclude my remarks by briefly touching on some specific issues relevant to the priestly ministry in the United States.

1. *Priestly Associations*. To combat the isolation of priests from one another, the *Code of Canon Law* (c. 278) recommends priestly associations which "promote holiness in the exercise of their ministry and foster the unity of the clergy with one another and with their bishop." Thus, the fostering of these

kinds of priestly associations is highly desirable, whereas those should not be allowed which do not contribute to the true formation and mission of the priest and which do not encourage loyal collaboration with the hierarchy.

2. *Impact of the prevailing culture.* The hedonism and consumeristic spirit which dominate Western society, and hence also the United States, impose a clearly materialistic scale of values, at the top of which are success, power, money, and pleasure. This is a great challenge for priests, as they must oppose this with a very different and more demanding hierarchy of values. Thus, it is not surprising to find examples of compromise or capitulation in the area of Catholic moral teaching and practice regarding sexuality, family life, and the common good.

3. *The rapport with priests from ethnic minorities.* Differences of language, culture, mentality, and traditional pastoral approaches are sometimes the source of misunderstandings and tensions, which must be overcome in the spirit of priestly fraternity. It should be recognized that minority priests are essential for the integration of their fellow countrymen into parochial life in North America.

4. *The relationship between priests and laity.* The situation as a whole does not pose serious problems, but there have been some tensions and misunderstandings arising, on the one hand, from an unwillingness of some priests to involve the laity in legitimate ways in pastoral activity and, on the other hand, from the desire of some to entrust the laity with responsibilities which really belong to priests. The bishops are called to educate both priests and laity to cooperate with each other in a healthy and orderly way.

Bernard Cardinal Law

Three priests are in mind as I write these words. The first, ordained 45 years and a most effective pastor, speaks of his ministry today in most favorable terms by comparison with the life and ministry of priests at the time of his ordination. With enthusiasm he speaks of his expanding role as spiritual director, the closeness to those whom he serves as pastor, and a deeper sense of communion with his bishop.

The second, a young man beginning his fourth year as a priest, writes glowingly of his full and fulfilling life of priestly ministry, revealing the secret of his happiness in the sense of community and of support he receives from his brother priests in the rectory.

The third, a man not yet 50, from his hospital bed where he struggles with cancer, reveals the depth of his commitment to priestly life and his greater pain for not being able to celebrate Mass.

These priests are not atypical. They are symbolic of the thousands of faithful priests who are extraordinarily effective agents of evangelization in a culture which has seen dramatic changes over the past 25 years, changes which have posed new challenges to the Church.

The number of those who have left active ministry is well known. The difficulty which our culture has in appreciating celibacy—or marriage, for that matter—has been well publicized. These and other pressures which might negatively impact priestly morale have been extensively noted and deserve serious consideration. What these factors can easily obscure, however, is that the priests of the United States are an extraordinarily faithful group of priests who have been called to evangelize in uniquely challenging times and have done so effectively. Every bishop in the United States, I feel certain, would echo these sentiments.

Priests as Evangelizers

The observance of Lent in our dioceses has been enriched, thanks to the work of so many dedicated priests, by the rites of Christian initiation. The four stages of that process—evangelization, catechesis, enlightenment, and a reflection on our life as Church—can be used to characterize four dimensions of priestly ministry: evangelizer, teacher, spiritual director, and church leader.

Evangelizer

Taking the Second Vatican Council as a point of departure, the priests as evangelizers in the Church have been pivotal in a liturgical renewal which has seen a change to the vernacular and a more ready access of priests and people to God's Word, a diversification of liturgical roles and a fuller and more active participation of the laity. A gauge of the enormous change for the good, a change in which priests have been key, will be the celebration of the Easter Vigil this year. Thousands of adults will be baptized and other thousands received into full communion. This highlight of the church year, which not so long ago was often celebrated in the obscurity of a few people early Holy Saturday morning, has been restored to its rightful place in the liturgical life of the Church—and this has been due in no small measure to our priests.

The priest, evangelizing through his preaching, is more rooted in Sacred Scripture, often engages in prayerful reflection with other priests in preparation of homilies, and is constantly challenged to respond to difficult questions of the times.

Teacher

Adult religious education at the parish level has developed greatly. Priests have been actively involved in preparing laity for their engagement in the imparting of Christian doctrine.

The seminary study has rendered a positive service to the renewal of seminary life. Programs of the continuing education and formation of priests continue to develop. The custom of sabbaticals for priests in pastoral ministry appears to be gaining.

Spiritual Leader

The priest evangelizes as a spiritual leader. An earlier image of the pastor as administrator, as a "brick and mortar" man, is being replaced by the image of the spiritual director, spiritual leader—"pastor"—if you will. The priest's own ongoing spiritual formation is an important factor in this development. It is significant that during the past two decades two programs of priestly renewal begun by priests in the United States have had national and international extension: the Emmaus Program and Father Dwyer's Program of Priestly Renewal. Increasing numbers of priests avail themselves of directed retreats in the classical Ignatian sense.

Church Leader

As a church leader, the priest has effectively evangelized by contributing to a growing sense of the Church as *communio*. This is demonstrated by the growth in the experience of communion with his local bishop. A more fraternal style facilitates this. Presbyteral councils have had a positive effect. Greater lay involvement in the life of the parish, a heightened concern for the role of women, and a growing appreciation that all are called to participate in the mission of the Church by virtue of baptism and confirmation have been furthered by priestly leadership. The priest has been important to the growth of spiritual movements like Cursillo, Marriage Encounter, Teens Encounter Christ, the Charismatic Movement, and many others. A greater sense of stewardship on the part of the laity is a tribute to the leadership of priests and is a further indication of a growing sense of the Church. Priests today are generally more conscious of the social doctrine of the Church and evangelize by opening hearts to the wider responsibilities of Christian discipleship.

Cultural Challenges

General Culture

There are certain aspects of contemporary U.S. culture which can be problematic for the Church as she seeks to evangelize. Because the priest is consistently dealing with these cultural issues in the day-to-day exercise of his ministry, he bears the burdens of these cultural challenges most acutely. In assessing the challenges which the Church faces in her evangelizing mission in the United States, it is helpful always to remember that the incarnational principle is key for evangelization. The Word became flesh and, in that incarnation, transformed flesh. The faith is to evangelize the culture and in doing so will be interwoven with that culture transformed. It is also good to remember that culture does not exist in a vacuum. It is encountered in individual human beings, in their relationships, in the institutions which mark their lives. Finally, I believe there can be a faulty premise in assessing the contemporary Church by assuming that the Church in the United States of 50 years ago was a golden era of Catholicism. While we might be inclined to look back with envy at an era of greater numbers and much expansion, the reality calls for greater analysis. To what extent was this growth carried by the culture or to what extent did it express a vibrant, internalized faith? The answer is not totally one or the other, but would more likely indicate that as earlier growth was not altogether due to a more vibrant faith, neither is later reduction due to a lessening faith. It is impossible to measure statistical highs or lows of church life apart from an analysis of culture.

Solipsism is a thread in contemporary culture. This is seen in the exaggerated emphasis on the right to privacy and a commensurate diminution in the recognition of the claims of the common good. The corresponding social ideal is, then, for voluntary organizations to an extent that such basic relationships as marriage and family are undermined precisely because of their permanence and the personal sacrifice they imply for the good of others.

Feminism has brought to greater consciousness, and happily so, the fundamental equality of women and men; it has stimulated a redress of economic and legal inequities and has brought about an expanded role for women in Church and society. It has been less positive, however, in its difficulty to appreciate complimentarity because of its tendency to view *difference* and *equality* as mutually exclusive.

The sexual revolution has isolated sexual pleasure as an end in itself and presents such pleasure as a right which the individual can exercise in whatever way he or she chooses. This is broadly stated, but accurately reflects a contemporary phenomenon. These problematic aspects arise out of an intellectual climate which eschews absolutes and a moral climate which exalts as virtue a non-judgmental acceptance of another's moral choices.

Within the Church

These cultural factors have obvious effect on the life of the Church. Theological dissent, doubts about celibacy, and difficulty with the Church's teaching on women's ordination are variations on these cultural themes. The priest has the daily pressure of dealing with these. He also suffers from a certain confusion within the

Church concerning the priesthood arising out of a failure to distinguish clearly the concepts of the priesthood, of the baptized, ministry, and orders.

Evangelization

The urgent call to the priest as evangelizer is seen in the large number of Catholics not being reached as well as in the millions of unchurched in our country. The priest must be sufficiently free of administrative tasks to meet this challenge and to call more effectively the faithful to their role as evangelizers.

Teaching

The priest as evangelizer is inhibited today to the extent that the Church may not be the principal teacher in his life. When other sources (psychology, sociology, politics, a theology of dissent, or whatever) become the primary guide for the vision, understanding, hopes, and ideals of the priest, he is not effective, obviously, in his proper role as teacher within the Church.

The faithful are often not practically or intellectually engaged by the Church. This task is incumbent on the priest not only as an evangelizer of individuals but also as an evangelizer of culture. We have yet to find suitable ways of conveying difficult truths to the men and women of today. A sometimes misinformed, often aggressive, all-pervasive media further blunts the effectiveness of the Church in this area.

Spiritual Life

The recognition of sin and, therefore, an appreciation of the sacrament of penance do not come easily in the moral climate of relativism. The ongoing conversion of the priest presupposes in him a firm conviction that Jesus reveals to us both God and what it means to be fully human, a sense of sin, a recognition of God's merciful love, and a frequent reception of penance. Only in this way can the priest be effective in calling others to conversion of heart and to the worthy reception of penance. The reality of the culture today makes the celibate witness much more difficult, but also much more important. Priests must be supported in dealing with the sacrifices of that witness, which has become more demanding in an increasingly couple-oriented or homosexual society. The

principal reason given for the early mass of petitions for laiciza-
tion was, "he does not have friends." There remain among active
priests many who are isolated from affective relations with others,
unable to give to and draw from others needed support and love.
Some lack a sense of "friendship" with their ministry; they cannot
give to and draw from their prayer and their mission the sense of
goodness and life which will sustain them well.

Church Life

The priest is called to a public role in making the Church present
in the wider society. This public aspect of the Church's mission is
made more difficult in a society which tends to excessively
privatize religion. The priest and future priests must possess a
clear understanding of the unique role of the priest in the Church
and in the Church's mission in the world while, at the same time,
maintaining flexibility in nonessentials which the current and
foreseeable future situation of the Church demand. The shortage
in vocations remains a pressing concern. The key to vocation
promotion is the happiness of the priests, seen in their lives and
in their work. Some, in their own unhappiness, have neither the
capacity nor the will to invite others to follow in the path they have
chosen.

Bishops as Teachers of the Faith

It is difficult to establish a sense of priestly identity in a culture
which often does not support the values of the Church. It is, therefore, all the more notable that so many thousands of priests have
a clear commitment to their life and ministry. It is, however, our
role as bishops to give direction and guidance to their efforts and
to provide the necessary assistance that the priests' service as
evangelizers in the Church meet the above-mentioned challenges
successfully.

Priests, Men of the Church

As bishops, we must help the priest to be a man with a deep
sense of the Church. The unique, sacramental relationship of
bishops and presbyters must find ever clearer and more effective
expression. There is always the danger that this reality be

obscured in an otherwise laudable effort to expand the participation of others in the mission of the church. Bishops, together with priests, have a primary role in diocesan life. This relationship depends not only on such structures as the presbyteral council, but also on the kind of human interaction that takes place between bishop and priest as well as among the priests.

Priests, Spiritual Leaders

The bishop must promote the spiritual life of the priest and encourage him to assume ever more effectively his role as spiritual leader. There must be recognition of the priority of the priest's relationship with God.

We as bishops can help priests assume their roles as spiritual leaders to the extent that we ourselves are and are perceived as such. We need to be men of prayer ourselves and to share that prayer with those with whom we are privileged to serve. The Chrism Mass will offer us a splendid opportunity for this.

Priests, Teachers of Faith

If we are to help priests to evangelize more effectively as teachers, it is necessary to bring the church into clearer focus as the principal teacher for the person of faith. Too easily today do we put the Church's teaching on a par with other voices. Too easily can the tendency of morality by polls have its effects on all of us, to the point that adherence to church teaching is weakened or its proclamation is uncertain. We need, as priests and bishops, an honest and vigorous theological engagement, not abstracting from the Church's teaching, but rooted in the Church's teaching.

Priests, Evangelizers

The priest is an effective evangelizer in our culture to the extent that he is a faith-filled man of the Church, a man rooted in the Lord and an able spiritual leader, a man who has made the "good news" expressed in Scripture and tradition the guide of his life, action, and teaching. To the extent that we are the same as bishops, to that extent do we support our brother priests in their task. I end as I began, with the encouraging vision of three priests representing three generations, faithfully and happily living out their vocations. Such are the evangelizers which the Church has in her service today and which her mission will more and more require.

The Pastoral Responsibility of Bishops Relative to Religious Life in the United States of America

Jean Jerome Cardinal Hamer

I.

The role of the bishop is to proclaim the Gospel, to convert souls to the Gospel. He will necessarily give special attention to those who wish to base their lives on the profession of evangelical counsels. These counsels are "evangelical" because they are a radical way of living the Gospel.

The bishop, therefore, is responsible not only for the apostolate of men and women religious (regarding their schools, their hospitals, catechesis, parish assistance, etc.) but also, to a certain extent, for their religious life as such. That is, he must oversee their observance of chastity, poverty, and obedience; their fraternal life in community; the witness they must bear to God before the people of God; and their fidelity to their distinct charism, which ought to place its stamp on all religious life.

It might be objected that men and women religious have their own juridical status, which sets them apart from the authority of the bishops. It is true that history and the law grant true autonomy of life to religious institutes and that bishops are supposed to defend and protect it (see c. 586). But it should be noted that this autonomy of life and government, which allows institutes to observe their own discipline and to preserve intact their own character and specific role, does not place members of religious orders outside the life of the diocese. On the contrary, it determines their mode of insertion in the life of the local Church.

II.

How is the bishop to assume this role vis-à-vis religious life? First, and above all, through his teaching. It is the bishop's task to introduce religious life in his diocese and to instill respect for it. This requires a broad range of information and great attention to religious life in catechesis, preaching, in the formation of future priests, and in any pastoral letters he may write.

The proper formation of priests is particularly important to the future of religious life. They will be the spiritual directors of the men and women religious and of young candidates for religious life. They will also be the chaplains of convents and monasteries, and future episcopal vicars.

The bishop is also responsible for the pastoral care of vocations. These arise in families, parishes, schools, apostolates, diocesan organizations, etc.

The bishop will also show his interest in religious life by choosing the appropriate people to represent him in dealing with the institutions and people. I am thinking here of the bishop's vicars and delegates for religious life.

It is also the bishop's job to welcome and assist nascent forms of religious life. He should, moreover, make the effort to discern the new gifts and new forms of consecrated life that the Holy Spirit entrusts to the Church (see c. 605).

All of these initiatives of the bishop (as well as those clearly defined under the law) will allow religious institutes to find their place in the life of the diocese—an insertion within the living fabric of the local community which is not just juridical, but also psychological and truly human.

In this regard, our Congregation would like to express its gratitude for all that the episcopate of the United States is doing to help men and women religious who have reached retirement age. Thanks to the efforts of the bishop, the diocese can also become a place of encounter, of constructive exchange, and an example for the different religious families.

Monasteries for nuns who are pledged to the contemplative life will be the object of particular attention on the part of the bishop. Canon law entrusts them to his care in a very special way. We have not spoken here of secular institutes and societies of apostolic life because that is not directly the object of this meeting, but it goes without saying that they fall within the bishop's field of service.

III.

On April 3, 1983, in a letter addressed to the bishops of the United States, the Holy Father established a special three-member commission headed by Archbishop John R. Quinn of San Francisco, whose purpose was to "facilitate the pastoral efforts of their brother bishops in the United States in helping the religious of your country whose institutes are engaged in apostolic works to live their ecclesial vocation to the full."

In doing so, John Paul II did not confer a new mandate on the bishops nor did he give them new powers. He simply highlighted the powers they already have in the carrying out of their pastoral office.

This letter and the good work of the pontifical commission served as the starting point for a new awareness of the type of pastoral service that the bishops can and should render to religious life. The dialogue that was begun in the various dioceses proved fruitful for all concerned. It has permitted many bishops to regain contact, under a new form, with the totality of religious life in their dioceses. It has also made it possible for many men and women religious to rediscover the reality of the particular Church, which they have had a tendency to forget.

Now our gaze is directed to the future. This pastoral service of religious life must be not only pursued, but intensified. We must exercise it within the framework of the actual situation of the Church in the United States.

Are we sufficiently prepared for this task? Are we sufficiently disposed? At any rate, it is a task we must assume together: each bishop in his diocese with his clergy, his men and women religious, and all the faithful; the bishops in fraternal collaboration among themselves; and with the Holy See, which is and wants to be always and above all at your service.

James Cardinal Hickey

1. Introduction

The vowed consecrated life is a precious gift which the Holy Spirit has given to the Church. The history of the Church in the United States is intimately tied to the arrival and growth of religious communities, from the coming of the first religious in the 16th century until today when new expressions of consecrated life are developing in our country. The Church in the United States was built on the generous service of these religious sisters, brothers, and priests who continue even today to staff hospitals, schools, colleges, and universities, and who provide a range of social services too numerous to list in this presentation. As bishops we are indebted to our religious for their holiness of life and service to the Church.

Like many other institutions of our time, religious life is in a period of transition, one that is often marked by pain and interior searching for the meaning of religious life. As in the past, the Church must authenticate and sustain this gift of the Spirit and keep it vigorously alive.

These reflections naturally bring to mind the experience of our American bishops during the course of the work of the pontifical commission headed by Archbishop John Quinn. It was a time of intense study and discussion beneficial to the Church in our country. My task is to offer a brief overview of the current situation of institutes of religious life dedicated to the works of the apostolate. Some of you, personally long experienced in living the religious life, will surely have information and insights to round out my brief outline.

2. Statistics

In 1965, there were 217,921 professed sisters, brothers, and priests in the United States. By 1975, that number had dropped to 166,134. The pattern has continued in the last decade: sisters (1978): 129,391; (1988): 106,912; brothers (1978): 8,460; (1988): 7,069; priests (1978): 22,719; (1988): 18,731 (1988 *Official Catholic Directory*). This dramatic decline is one indicator of the crisis which many religious congregations in the United States are facing. As overall membership declines at an alarming rate, fewer candidates present themselves and even fewer persevere. The average age of religious has risen sharply in the last 20 years, and the needs of retired religious have become a serious concern for the Church in the United States.

3. Influences

Permit me now to identify some elements in our culture affecting religious life in recent years.

a) *The instability of family life*. It is estimated that one out of every two marriages ends in divorce. The breakdown of the nuclear and extended family is well documented. As a result, many young people lack a clear value system or a strong sense of personal morality. This often hinders them from making permanent life commitments.

b) *A strong spirit of democracy*. This is basic to American life and one of our greatest blessings. But some expect all church structures to conform to the democratic structures so common in American life. When a difference is perceived, some are led to mistrust and even reject legitimate church authority.

c) *An exaggerated confidence in science and technology*. This has tended to result in widespread skepticism and agnosticism, tendencies often strongest among the youth of our nation.

d) *An overreliance on the social sciences*. These sciences, particularly psychology, often shape the values and norms of our society. For many Americans, volunteerism and a multitude of self-help programs take the place religion used to occupy.

There are other cultural elements which affect religious life in our country more directly. These include:

a) Many people reach adulthood with a poorly formed faith. Too many do not know what the Church teaches nor do they consider God an important part of their lives. A firm foundation in faith is absolutely necessary for living the vocation of religious life.

b) During the last quarter of a century, the Church in the United States has experienced a period of ideological and religious pluralism unknown in our earlier history. Within the same religious institute divergent views have arisen on many seminal issues which previously bound members closely together. These issues include the centrality of living in community, the value of various religious practices, and the authority of the ordinary magisterium. In some cases the very meaning of vowed religious life and its relationship to the Church, both local and universal, remain points of disagreement and even division among members of the same institute.

c) The current emphasis on justice issues and concern for social needs has profoundly affected the way religious view themselves and their ministries. Strains of liberation theology have prompted some religious to place heavy emphasis on the need to redress social injustice by engaging in political activism. In consequence, some place much less emphasis on the transcendent nature of religious life.

d) The feminist critique strongly influences the way some religious men and women understand, experience, and evaluate their calling.

4. Current Emphases

At the present time, I see two basic orientations with regard to religious life: the first stresses mission and ministry; the second stresses consecration and community. I hasten to add that neither group intends to emphasize one aspect of religious life to the exclusion of the other.

a) The focus on mission seems characteristic of the majority of religious institutes of men and women in the United States. Since the Council, these institutes have stressed the importance of being in the midst of the world in order to address its needs. Consequently, the external structures of religious life are de-emphasized with a view toward immersion in ministry. Indeed some religious describe the fundamental purpose of religious life as "community for mission." Small communities or living alone in apartments is sometimes chosen as a way of drawing close to those who are to be served. Choosing one's ministry in consultation with superiors replaces direct assignment. In some few cases religious engage in works not specifically related to the Church. Some institutes have turned from corporate commitments such as teaching and health care in order to work on social justice issues. They perceive a need to become more politically effective in both church and civic communities. Many religious are convinced they are developing new forms of religious life while at the same time living in a manner consonant with membership in an approved religious institute.

b) A second approach focuses on consecration through the vows as a value in itself and as a basis for community apostolate. This view represents a smaller percent of institutes, sometimes described as "traditional" or "conservative." Some groups, though not all, draw a steady stream of candidates. Nevertheless, such groups often feel they are a minority whose views are not adequately considered. They see continuity with the past as necessary for future growth. They look to the magisterium and their own traditions to determine future directions. These groups believe religious consecration is nurtured by the external structures of conventual living; they maintain and emphasize the centrality of common life, common prayer, the religious habit, and community-based ministries. The role of the superior remains fundamental to their notion of religious obedience. Above all, these religious stress the transcendent nature of the consecrated religious life even as they serve human needs here and now.

5. The Bishop and Religious Life

In this challenging time for religious, what are our most basic reponsibilities as bishops? I see five basic duties. First, it is the duty of the bishop, in union with the Holy Father, to preserve, develop, and defend religious life as a precious gift for the whole Church. We must continually share the teaching of the Church on the nature, and purpose of consecrated life and resist ideologies and trends which contradict its true nature. Today we need to defend the Christological character of religious life, its transcendent nature, and the centrality of the evangelical counsels of poverty, chastity, and obedience. We need to point out the value of consecrated life in and of itself, independent of the works in which religious are engaged. We must also stress the importance of community life and the need for some distinctive sign of consecration as indicative of those values. Religious life is countercultural, a sign of contradiction.

As bishops we must continue to develop an ever deeper and more precise understanding of religious life, reflecting with care on the teaching of the Holy See and listening attentively to the experience of our religious, who have persevered through a time of unprecedented change. We need the continuing guidance of our Holy Father to refocus the tradition of religious life for our times and to rediscover the matrix of religious life, from which a multitude of institutes and apostolic works has sprung.

Second, it is our responsibility to reflect on the relationship between the bishop and the religious present in his diocese. The bishop must respect the unique charism of each institute even as he invites religious to be his collaborators in the work of evangelization. To achieve such an appreciation, we must spend time with the religious serving our local churches, meet with them, and learn of their experience of the Church and community life. This ongoing exchange between ourselves and religious communities is important for mutual understanding and effective cooperation in the work of spreading the Gospel.

Greater clarity is also needed in the matter of the relationship between the bishop and religious institutes of "pontifical right." In addition, the phenomenon of new communities requires of the bishop a careful study of their charism and constitutions. All such charisms must be at the service of the whole Church. Religious life cannot be independent from the bishop nor indifferent to the hierarchy.

Third, we must help to strengthen communications among all religious and the Holy See. The Leadership Conference of Women Religious and the Conference of Major Superiors of Men are currently the only official channels between the Holy See and religious women and men in our country. For a variety of reasons, these organizations do not represent the views and concerns of all religious institutes in the United States. A significant number of religious relate to the *Consortium Perfectae Caritatis* or the Institute on Religious Life. I see a need for us as bishops to foster discussion at the local and the universal level among religious holding divergent points of view. We should also remember that many religious women not represented by the LCWR desire some representation with the Holy See.

Fourth, as pastors we need to hold up to the young the highest esteem for religious life and invite them to consider this calling. We must teach priests and seminarians the important role and worth of the religious life and urge them to work for vocations.

Fifth, we should assist religious when they face immediate and pressing problems such as the need for money to care for their elderly and retired members; the need for more effective recruitment; the need to offer adequate compensation to religious for their apostolic labors. In the United States we have begun to address these issues; our support and encouragement must continue.

6. Some Important Questions

In view of the developments with regard to religious life in the United States, how should bishops respond to the questions and initiatives which religious are themselves considering?

How can we help our religious to be faithful to their identity in a rapidly shifting culture?

How can we act as a bridge between religious of divergent emphases for the unity of the Church?

What is our response to those who speak to us about the "refoundation" of their religious institutes?

What is our response to the many new foundations, emerging sometimes from already long-established congregations?

What is our response to the proposal that some religious communities become secular institutes or a new form of consecrated life?

How can we develop an awareness among our young people of the value of a religious vocation today, especially among our Hispanic, Black, and Asian Catholics?

Surely we can answer these questions only out of a united conviction about the nature and purpose of apostolic religious life, a view of religious as persons consecrated in a public way to Jesus Christ and charged with the work of spreading the Gospel to our brothers and sisters everywhere.

Today religious men and women face a fundamental challenge clearly identified by our Holy Father in his 1980 address to religious men in São Paulo—the challenge of being integrated with those to be served "without hiding or disguising the specific originality of [their] vocation: to follow Christ, poor, chaste and obedient." May we as bishops draw our religious men and women ever closer to the teaching and inner life of the Church even as they strive to respond in fidelity and joy to the challenges of our culture.

Liturgy and the Sacraments, with Particular Emphasis upon the Sacrament of Reconciliation

Eduardo Cardinal Martinez Somalo

In John Paul II's letter *Dominicae Cenae*, it was reaffirmed that "a very close and organic bond exists between the renewal of the liturgy and the renewal of the whole life of the Church. The Church not only acts but also expresses herself in the liturgy, lives by the liturgy and draws from the liturgy the strength for her life."

We are all convinced that the liturgical reform has been one of the great gifts of the Spirit to the Church. This gift has been put into the hands of priests by the Church as a treasure to be made available to the faithful.

From this premise is derived the following consequence. No liturgical action can be considered a private action: each celebration belongs to the Church, the sacrament of unity. Therefore, each liturgical action should be treated in harmony with the indications given by the Church, without taking liberties by adding, taking away, or changing anything in any way according to the rules of one's own fantasy. This will guarantee respect for the rites themselves, assure the validity of the sacraments, and show respect for the religious feeling of the faithful.

A glance at the liturgical life of the Church of America is offered by the Holy See on the basis of the following elements:

- from direct correspondence between the Congregation for Divine Worship and the Sacraments and the presidents of the bishops' conference and of the Bishops' Committee on the Liturgy;
- from direct contact with the Bishops' Committee on the Liturgy and with its secretariat in Washington, D.C.;
- from the biannual visits of the president, vice president, and general secretary of the United States bishops' conference;

- from information gathered from the official monthly newsletter;

- from the *Ad Limina* visits (during the past year, many bishops have come in person to the Congregation and met with the officials of the dicastery. More than 200 five-year reports were subsequently examined and each one answered);

- from requests for information on the part of individual bishops; and

- from letters from priests and lay faithful asking for information or for clarification or even complaining about abuses.

The principal points emerging from the above-mentioned sources are the following:

- At the beginning of liturgical reform, a great work of grassroots catechesis was done in the United States through directives, norms, and instructions. These documents were outstanding both in number and in quality. This work has continued in subsequent years up to the present time.

- Liturgical reform has been generally accepted in the United States. But there was frequent reaction from minority groups, which though very small were very vocal. Public opinion has been their sounding board.

- Diocesan liturgical commissions have been the tools in the bishops' hands. In general, these commissions have been well led by priests specialized in liturgy (with a license or degree), and they have done a good job of giving instruction on innovations in the liturgical world and training priests and lay people.

- It is very positive to note that the bishops are vitally aware of the need to continue the ongoing formation of the clergy and faithful in liturgical matters. Efforts are now being directed toward a deeper study of the texts and rites.

- It is providential that a great effort has been directed toward meeting the linguistic needs of the many diverse groups existing in the United States. I have been told that in some cities Sunday Mass is celebrated in as many as 20 different languages.

Difficulties Encountered

In the midst of so much positive progress, certain obstacles have been encountered along the way that have made it more difficult to maintain a unity of discipline. It becomes a particularly delicate matter when it concerns that celebration in which *congregavit nos Christi amor*: that is, when it deals with the celebration of the Eucharist. There have been problems of interpretation as to the procedures to be followed regarding experiments in liturgical matters. The attention of all the episcopal conferences was drawn to this matter in the declaration of March 21, 1988: "Experiments in liturgical matters, when necessary or at least opportune, are authorized only by this sacred congregation, in writing, using precise and fixed rules, and under the responsibility of the competent local authority." A difficulty could arise when the bishops do not exercise their authority in a timely way in the liturgical field, a responsibility which *Christus Dominus* spells out when it affirms: "It is therefore bishops who are the principal dispensers of the mysteries of God, and it is their function to control, promote and protect the entire liturgical life of the Church entrusted to them" (no. 15). It is the duty of the national liturgical commission to express the mind of the bishops and to translate what they intend into practice.

In the English-speaking world the problem of "exclusive language" has arisen. Some have seen in it a discrimination with regard to women. In 1980, some conferences proposed certain changes in the eucharistic prayers and other liturgical texts in order to address this problem. But the problem remains unresolved because it is not only a question of grammatical agreement of gender, but also touches on biblical and theological questions as well and must be treated by different congregations.

In the delegation of "extraordinary" ministers of the Eucharist, the aspect of "service" to be given to the community should prevail; the ministry is not a prize to be given to a person nor a way of solemnizing a celebration. I would like to repeat what has been communicated to all the bishops' conferences: that these ought to remain extraordinary and to function only when ordinary ministers (i.e., bishops, priests, deacons) are not present in sufficient numbers.

At times some have questioned the validity or applicability of liturgical norms. The most frequent issue is that of women serving directly at the altar (acolyte): the idea has been spread that the instruction *Inaestimabile Donum*, (no. 18), is no longer a binding norm. When the Congregation is asked about this, it can only answer that the norm remains in force *donec aliter provideatur* (until otherwise provided).

A Look at the Sacraments

Having looked at liturgical celebrations in general, let us now glance at the strictly sacramental aspect. A general look at the documentation received from the American bishops permits us to see that pastoral programs relative to the celebrations of the sacraments are centered on certain areas that speak of a preoccupation of a pastoral nature: of catechesis regarding the preparation for reception of the sacraments in order, of participation, and, finally, of the vital dimension: how to live the sacraments that have been received.

Let us look at some of them.

The Eucharist

The Mass is the principal liturgical celebration of the Church: "No Christian community is built up which does not grow from and hinge on the celebration of the most holy Eucharist" (*Presbyterorum Ordinis*, 6). In the United States, as in the whole Church, the Mass is the object of much pastoral attention. The use of the missal authorized by Vatican II gives us the possibility of a deeper understanding of the Word of God through the selection of the readings, and of enrichment by the eucharistic prayer through the four prayers of the missal. The pastoral task lies in having eucharistic celebrations that show faith in the action of Christ, who gives to the Church his paschal sacrifice. Through them the faithful are helped to understand the word and are encouraged to participate through appropriate homilies. All this takes place in a festive atmosphere, in harmony with the "feast of the Lord." This is not the same atmosphere as that of profane feasts: it ought clearly to have the image of action filled with that sacredness proper to the Eucharist, as Pope John Paul II described years ago in his letter *Dominicae Cenae.*

The Congregation shares with the American bishops the preoccupation over certain eucharistic celebrations in which this sacredness seems less evident. Personal and group initiatives take precedence over the rites of the Church, and sometimes the prayers that express the faith of the Church undergo modifications. There is also concern for those groups which distance themselves from the present liturgy and raise objections, even of a doctrinal nature, against the current liturgical books using the pretext of the "traditional" Mass. The permanent sacramental presence of the Lord in the tabernacle remains in our churches as the fruit of the eucharistic celebration. Adoration of the Eucharist is a privileged form of prayer and an aid to Christian spirituality. It is a pastoral area that the bishops of the United States are not neglecting.

Penance

Together with the Eucharist, penance is the sacrament that accompanies us habitually along this path we are following as saints and sinners in the Church. Penitential discipline is one of the duties most tied traditionally to the episcopal office. The problems that have appeared over the years around the sacrament of reconciliation are not taken lightly by the bishops' conference of the United States nor by the Congregation.

The problem of the sacrament of reconciliation is not only a ritual problem. But a more accurate application of the present rite, with its own dynamic, would lead more easily to an establishment of the sacrament of penance along the lines indicated in the exhortation, *Reconciliatio et Paenitentia.* At any rate, what is fundamental in this area is the unity of discipline. Without this, the faithful fall into confusion, which either leads them to look for the easiest way out or brings them to a crisis over the very use of the sacrament.

Every five-year report shows serious pastoral concerns over the sacrament of reconciliation. These arise from the conviction that the sense of sin is being lost.

At the plenary meeting of our Congregation, held in April 1986, Pope John Paul II, referring specifically to this sacrament, recommended the organization of courses to update priests in the administration of this sacrament.

The ongoing instruction of the clergy and of the faithful on the nature of this sacrament should lead all to appreciate its multiple benefits, discovering that it is "not only an obligation, but also a true and proper right" (cf. 1986 plenary meeting). I would also like to refer to the ecclesiastical discipline regarding the order of first confession and first communion, even though the permission given for experimentation expired back in July 1973.

The Holy Father noted that "things had reached a point where people had lost sight of the great help that an appropriate administration of this sacrament can give even to children in their progressive and harmonious growth of conscience and dominion over themselves, in the willingness to accept themselves with their limitations, without at the same time passively resigning themselves to them." The practice of general absolution is included within this area of concern. Even if legitimate in specific circumstances, it is clear that a too common use of this form of celebration can become less educative of the sense, both personal and ecclesial, of the confession of sins.

The episcopal conference has established one month for the *diu*, the length of time during which penitents would have to be deprived of the grace of the sacrament and which would permit the authorization for imparting collective absolution when the other conditions are also present (cf. c. 961). We have noted with satisfaction that pastoral letters and instructions of some bishops declared that in their territory at the present time there are no cases in which the conditions for authorizing collective absolution could be foreseen.

The most important pastoral task we have today regarding the sacrament of penance is to succeed in making it a moment of experience, in faith, of the mercy of the Father who brings us the joy of return. For the Christians of our cities, subjected to so many pressures, it should be possible to make of the sacrament of penance that moment in which God restores the people to themselves and gives them pardon and peace through the ministry of the Church.

Other Sacraments

Now is not the time to refer to the whole field of pastoral work. We are the dispensers of these "humble and precious sacraments" (cf. *Reconciliatio et Penitentia*), in which the Lord himself encounters people.We are not the masters of the sacraments, and when we celebrate them, we must all have the intention of doing what the Church does if they are to be truly efficacious. On the other hand, it is our pastoral duty to promote the personal faith of those who receive the sacraments, so that the sacramental act might have its full efficaciousness.

Holy Orders

Speaking of the sacrament of order, on the basis of experience, our Congregation would like to recommend that the greatest attention be given to the selection and preparation of the candidates both for the permanent diaconate and for the priesthood. In fact, the requests for dispensation are numerous.

Matrimony

All the five-year reports are very clear in stating the great effort made in the preparation for this sacrament, which is absolutely necessary in order that couples understand completely the obligations they are about to assume and will not be able to say later that they did not know about. As we well know, such a preparation includes a clear presentation of the doctrine of the magisterium on human life at every stage. Consequently, it is of great importance that priests be well instructed in the relevant doctrine of the Church. We share your profound concern for the great number of mixed marriages, in which every effort should be made to assure the faith of the Catholic partner and the corresponding education of the offspring.

Conclusion

The Congregation has had many occasions to express its appreciation for the work done in the renewal of the liturgy in the United States. There exists there a profound religious spirit, a love for the Church on the part of Catholics, and a great respect for it on the part of many non-Catholics. The eucharistic celebration has a central place in the life of the faithful. The willingness and generosity of the faithful are notable in every sector of ecclesial life. It would not be too much to say that a love for the liturgy exists in the United States.

Council texts have reaffirmed that it is the duty of the bishops to promote and guide liturgical life in their dioceses and to lead the priests wisely in the most opportune manner to respect the one discipline of the Church. This means that it is necessary to have the courage to act in a timely way when there is a need to resist that which is contrary to the laws and prescribed usage in the celebration of the liturgy. In this way, the faithful will not be disoriented by so-called abuses, and the celebration of the Mass will be a glory to God and useful to the Church. In this regard, please allow me to recall the recommendation made in the final report of the 1985 extraordinary Synod of Bishops: "The bishops should not merely correct abuses but should also clearly explain to everyone the theological foundation of the sacramental discipline and of the liturgy" (I, B, b, 2). This dicastry declares itself to be always at the service of the bishops' conference of the United States (cf. *Pastor Bonus*, 64.1), and it expresses the hope for an ever-growing spirit of fraternal collaboration in everything that might contribute to the divine worship and to the sacramental life of the people of God.

Archbishop Daniel Kucera, OSB

I have been asked to relate the strengths and weaknesses of the liturgical life of the Church in the United States of America. While it is impossible to give a comprehensive view of the American liturgical experience in ten minutes, I hope to touch the important liturgical issues facing us as we approach the 21st century.

During our recent *Ad Limina* visits, we, the bishops from the United States, reported on the state of the liturgical life in our individual dioceses. Without glossing over particular deficiencies, we can say that the overall national picture is gratifying.

The liturgical reforms instituted by the Second Vatican Ecumenical Council and promulgated and implemented by Pope Paul VI and by Your Holiness have been accepted by the large majority of Catholics in the United States. The spiritual significance of these reforms has been integrated into their personal lives as well as that of their parishes. Several examples bear this out.

The majority of American Catholics have developed a healthy and reverent understanding of the sacred rites of the Church and participate with devotion. At Sunday Eucharist, the Sacred Scriptures and the eucharistic sacrifice have enriched the everyday life of the faithful. Our people have been led to increased devotion, study, and commitment to the Gospel. Full, conscious, and active participation continues to bond Catholics together as one body eager for spiritual growth, committed to charitable service, and faithful to the teaching of the Church. Catholics actively participate in the celebration through the prayers and chants of the Mass which belong to them. Some with special gifts are trained to be readers, cantors, acolytes, liturgical musicians, ushers, and when needed, special ministers of holy communion. Most parishes have developed the ministries referred to in the *General Instruction of the Roman Missal*.

Attention is now being given in more and more parishes to refining the liturgical reforms. Parish liturgical committees, composed of members of the laity working alongside their priests, prepare for the Sunday Eucharist and other liturgical celebrations by giving special emphasis to the nature of the liturgical seasons, the quality of liturgical music, the composition of inspiring homilies, and the coordination of the various liturgical ministers. This careful preparation helps to produce more reverent and unified celebrations.

Nearly one-half of American Catholics attend Sunday Mass each week. The vast majority receive holy communion at these Masses. While this statistic shows a greater level of participation than in many other developed Western countries, we are seeking more effective ways of encouraging participation of nonpracticing Catholics. We remind those who do receive holy communion regularly of the need to be prepared spiritually for the reception of the sacrament of the Body and Blood of Christ.

Because of large numbers receiving holy communion on Sundays and because of the growing number of lay people who bring communion to the sick and the aged, it is necessary in most parishes to use special ministers of holy communion to assist the ordinary ministers of the parish. Many parishes offer holy communion under both kinds on Sundays and other occasions, in keeping with the special norms of *This Holy and Living Sacrifice,* approved by the Congregation for Divine Worship in 1984. In such cases, additional special ministers of holy communion are needed to distribute the Precious Blood.

The sacramental life of our parishes has been enriched greatly by the implementation of the *Rite of Christian Initiation of Adults.* A provisional translation of this ritual was in use for fourteen years before the final translation was published last year. Its rites, along with the restored catechumenate, are meeting the spiritual needs of a growing number of parishes and at the same time are a source of great spiritual blessing and renewal for local churches.

Baptismal preparation programs for parents of infants are now becoming the norm throughout the United States. A sincere attempt is made to ensure proper understanding of baptism so that children are raised in a life of Christian faith in the Church.

Both of these rituals and their associated formation programs are proving to be wonderful models for involvement of laity in the total spiritual development of the parish. They hold great promise because they emphasize the common responsibility of the faithful to share their faith as they bring others to Christ.

As bishops we are concerned that the revised *Rite of Penance* has met with less success than hoped. A recent survey conducted by the Bishops' Committee on Pastoral Research and Practices shows that 25 percent of practicing Catholics receive the sacrament of penance weekly, monthly, or every other month. Slightly more than half of all practicing Catholics receive the sacrament once or twice a year. But 19 percent of practicing Catholics—that is, those who regularly attend Sunday Mass and contribute financially to the support of the Church—report that they no longer have recourse to this sacrament. Involved here, of course, is the whole question of understanding the theology of sin and personal responsibility.

Many confessors have expressed the need to abbreviate the 1973 revised rite for individual reconciliation under pressure of time. Yet priests who have used the revised formulary find it has a truly positive effect. The restoration of this sacrament in the spiritual lives of our people poses a challenge that we bishops are addressing by our preaching and teaching.

The Rite for Reconciliation of Several Penitents with Individual Confession and Absolution has been pastorally effective. During Advent and Lent, most parishes celebrate communal penance services with several priests present as confessors. Many feel that this rite, which combines the personal intimacy of individual confession with the communal celebrations of repentance and reconciliation, gives particular attention to the role of the Church as a community wounded by sin and an effective sign of God's reconciling love. The Rite of Reconciliation of Several Penitents with General Confession and Absolution has been used quite sparingly in the United States, despite vocal but inaccurate claims to the contrary. Typically it has been used in circumstances where unexpectedly there were more than 100 penitents per available confessor. Data gathered in our survey shows that this form of the sacrament may have an important pastoral value as a means of reintroducing alienated Catholics to the life of the Church. This may be an area of future study. But certainly the celebration of this rite should always be limited to those extraordinary circumstances for which it was intended, and we are careful to forestall its use beyond the norms of law.

Over the past 25 years, we have witnessed in the United States liturgical abuses at both ends of the ideological spectrum. A very small portion of the Catholic faithful reject the reformed liturgy and refuse to implement the revised rites. Conversely, some have gone beyond the approved liturgical rites and introduced often questionable elements into the liturgy. Both extremes, we think, occur less frequently than in the past and should disappear as proper catechesis and training in liturgical observance continue.

67

The careful preparation of seminarians in understanding the proper role of one who presides over the liturgical prayer of the Church remains a critical need.

Most Catholics value the liturgical reforms. Being able to participate actively in the liturgy in their own language is greatly appreciated. It would seem incongruous and disturbing to most to return to liturgical forms which deprive them of worshiping as one community in their common language.Unfortunately, some letters addressed to the Apostolic See allege that liturgical abuses are widespread in the United States. In reality, this is not so. Those who complain often are objecting to things which are legitimate and approved. They are also looking for ways to discredit the present rites. So-called traditionalists repeatedly attack the authority of the diocesan bishops and the national episcopal conference and encourage disaffected individuals to write to the supreme pontiff and to the various congregations of the Roman Curia. Their problem often is not with the *liturgy*, but with Catholic *ecclesiology*.

Your Holiness, on several occasions during and after your pastoral visits to the United States, you referred to the vibrant celebrations of the Eucharist at which you presided. We are very grateful for this affirmation. We wish to emphasize that what you experienced takes place at the local level also. Throughout the United States, week after week, in parishes large and small, urban and rural, the liturgy of the Church is celebrated with reverence and love. The renewal of the liturgical life in the United States has been one of the greatest and most visible gifts that the Second Vatican Ecumenical Council has given to us. We feel the liturgy is both a source and a mirror of the spiritual vitality of the Church in the United States.

The Laity as Agents of Evangelization

Eduardo Cardinal Pironio

"The time has come to engage in a new evangelization" (*Christifideles Laici*, 34).

In light of the American bishops' *Ad Limina* visits—from the Holy Father's discourses on those occasions and from the quinquennial reports—and numerous other documents and contacts between our dicastery and the bishops of the United States, as well as in light of the apostolic exhortation *Christifideles Laici*, I would put forward some points for our dialogue.

The apostolic exhortation offers three main guidelines which may be taken as keys for discernment and orientation (on the bishops' part) in the pastoral care of the laity:

1. return attention and discussion of the formation and activity of the lay faithful within the perspective of the *call to holiness* (corresponds to the first chapter of *Christifideles Laici*, on the dignity—identity—of the lay faithful in the Church as mystery);

2. testify and educate toward a serene, firm, and joyful sense of belonging to the Church in all her greatness as *a mystery of communion* (corresponds to the second chapter, on the participation of the lay faithful in the life of the Church as communion);

3. promote a *new missionary zeal* in the lay faithful within the Church and within society (corresponds to the third chapter, on the coresponsibility of the lay faithful in the Church as mission).

These three guidelines—clearly developed by the Holy Father in his homily at the closing of the synod—were already present, in a sense, in the theme which Archbishop May presented to the synod as the result of the presynodal consultation: "Fellow Disciples of Christ in the Church's Mission in the World." On the other hand, these guidelines are directly inspired in the *Final Report of the 1985 Extraordinary Synod*: the Church as mystery, as communion, as mission.

1. *The dignity (or identity) of the lay faithful in the Church as mystery.* I propose to underline three basic aspects which call for special attention on the part of the bishops:

a) a positive description of the lay faithful: grounded in the "newness" of Christian life conferred by baptism (brought to maturity in the other sacraments of initiation) and their "secular character" (understood as a theological, not a sociological notion);

b) the call to holiness which is "rooted in Baptism and proposed anew in the other sacraments, principally in the Eucharist" (*Christifideles Laici*, 16), but which is realized and expressed in a particular way in involvement in temporal affairs and participation in earthly activities (cf. ibid., 17);

c) the requirement of an ongoing integral formation and the presentation of an authentic lay spirituality ("life according to the Spirit, in Christ," with a particular dimension that is secular or incarnational). The apostolic exhortation incorporates this synodal proposition: "the formation of the lay faithful must be placed among the priorities of a diocese . . . within the plan of pastoral action, that the efforts of the whole community (priests, laity, and religious) converge on this goal" (Proposition 40, *Christifideles Laici*, 57).

We can then examine:

• the completeness of the formation (participation in the mystery of Christ, social doctrine of the Church);

• the places or environment of that formation: the parish, the family, school, associations or movements, retreat houses;

• the agents of that formation: priests, men and women religious, lay persons, but above all the bishop, the principal agent of formation in the diocese (diocesan liturgies, preaching, pastoral letters).

A first conclusion: The bishop is the one primarily responsible for the sacramental (baptismal, Christian) awareness of the laity, of their spiritual growth into holiness, of their formation; for a "new evangelization."

2. *The participation of the lay faithful in the life of the Church as communion.* The principal innovation of *Christifideles Laici* is the presentation of the lay faithful's vocation and mission within an ecclesiology of communion, which was at the heart of the council and reproposed by the 1985 Extraordinary Synod. "Communion as the source and fruit of mission," as underlined in the 1987 Synod and as repeated in the apostolic exhortation (no. 32).

It is a question, above all, of that essential communion with the Father through Christ in the Holy Spirit; trinitarian communion and according to the model of the Trinity. Then it is a question of the organic communion of the people of God, presided over and guided by their pastors. I would wish to underline three points:

a) *Participation.* Grafted by baptism onto Christ, prophet, priest and king, and made living members of the very Body of Christ and God's people, the lay faithful share fully in the common dignity of all God's children, in the common call to holiness, and in the evangelizing mission common to the whole Church. However, it is not a sharing of a purely sociological or democratic kind, but a sharing sacramentally established on the apostolic and Petrine ministry, guarantee of the truth entrusted to that ministry, source of authentic freedom and communion. The experience of living in a democratic society where citizens assume responsibility for the life of their local community, in the world of business, in educational and cultural institutions, etc., can lead to adopting in the Church a sociological model of a human-historical democracy. The model of participation in the Church has a spiritual and theological dimension; and herein lies a special responsibility of the bishop. It is necessary to give particular importance to the normal channels of participation: pastoral councils (diocesan and parochial), councils of the laity at the national, diocesan, and parish levels.

b) *Ministries.* It might appear that the apostolic exhortation has been too restrictive or limited. Instead, I believe it is strongly encouraging. It is well known that in these 20 years of putting the council into practice there has been a widespread blossoming of non-ordained ministries both in the universal Church and, notably, in the Church in the United States. With gratitude to the Lord, the synod acknowledged this availability of the lay faithful for the various ministries, but it also called attention to the danger of a certain "inflation" of ministries and to the danger of a "clericalization" of the laity. Accepting the recommendation of the synod fathers, the Holy Father has set up a special commission "to provide an in-depth study of the various theological, liturgical, juridical, and pastoral considerations which are associated with the great increase today of the ministries entrusted to the lay faithful" (*Christifideles Laici*, 23).

c) *Associations and Movements*. It would seem important for the bishops to give special attention to the various forms of association adopted by the lay faithful which enrich the communion and mission of the Church, both traditional forms and those belonging to the new expanding ecclesial movements. In their regard the apostolic exhortation proposes clear "criteria of ecclesiality" (*Christifideles Laici*, 30) and recalls the unique responsibility of pastors in the service of discernment for communion (ibid., 31). It might prove useful to name some of the movements and groups most often referred to by the U.S. bishops: Cursillos, Charismatic Renewal, Knights of Columbus, Legion of Mary, Marriage Encounter.

3. *The coresponsibility of the lay faithful in the Church as mission*. The third chapter of *Christifideles Laici* opens with a very valuable comment on "mission to communion": "Communion and mission are profoundly connected with each other; they interpenetrate and mutually imply each other to the point that communion represents both the source and the fruit of mission: communion gives rise to mission and mission is accomplished in communion" (no. 32).

In this missionary perspective we can underline three points:

a) the engagement of the lay faithful in the new evangelization: explicit proclamation of Christ through the conversion of others and the building of a new society;

b) service to the human person and to society; the presence of the laity in the fields of economy and politics; the special responsibility of the Church in the United States in these areas both nationally and internationally. Without entering into detail regarding the important documents of the U.S. hierarchy on "peace" and "the economy," they show the

Church's presence in public life, ready to face the great questions and challenges of the life of the country and to contribute and promote newer solutions in the light of the Gospel and social doctrine. It is perhaps more difficult to indicate the existence in the country of a Catholic laity with a "national" presence and input, who give witness of a living synthesis between the faith they profess and their social, educational, cultural commitments in the world of business and labor, in political life, and in scientific endeavors. Concretely, during the synod Cardinal Bernardin observed: "The theology of the lay calling and the needs of politics require the direct commitment of the Church in the political order both through the lay faithful . . . strongly rooted in the Church's vision and teaching as well as in the art of politics and related matters . . . with the encouragement of the bishops in fulfilling this vocation";

c) finally, I wish to indicate briefly three categories of evangelizing agents among the lay faithful:

- the old and the sick: considered not only as objects of evangelization, but especially as its agents;
- women: fully incorporated into the Church's communion and mission, but without leaving doubts as to the Church's discipline regarding ordination;
- youth: they constitute a major priority in the pastoral ministry of John Paul II. Praiseworthy is the American bishops' concern in this area, and the Pontifical Council for the Laity—which has a special section for young people—is grateful for the excellent and accurate response given to the questionnaire sent out by our dicastery.

I conclude by indicating our sincere admiration for all that the U.S. bishops did in preparation for the Synod on the Laity. We are certain of their pastoral concern in making known and in applying the recent apostolic exhortation *Christifideles Laici*, which will be like a small *summa* for the Catholic laity. The Pontifical Council for the Laity is always available to receive the valuable suggestions of the bishops regarding the lay faithful and to accompany the efforts and joys of their pastoral ministry in this vast field, which is so rich and promising.

Archbishop Patrick Flores

I. Biblical Basis for Laity as Agents of Evangelization

A. The Gerasene Demoniac (Mk 5:1-20)

- The Lord crossed to the other side of the sea, going into the territory of the Gerasenes.

- Because of Jesus' initiative in meeting the demoniac where he was, seeing his need, and reaching out in compassion to him, the man with the demon experiences a freedom and healing not possible for him before.

- The man recognizes Jesus as the Reason/Cause for his new life and freedom and joy, and begs Jesus to let him accompany him in order to stay close to Him.

- Jesus refused, but told him instead to go home to his own family and people, and "tell them all that the Lord in his mercy has done for you." The Lord challenges the man to celebrate his new-found personal love and relationship with Jesus by going out to others, to those in his immediate environment, to those he lived and worked with in his ordinary everyday life.

- The man accepted Jesus' challenge, went off and began to proclaim in the Decapolis the wonderful work the Lord had done.

- People were amazed. What the man shared about his experience actually did touch his family and neighbors, and they all began to change as a result.

B. The Samaritan Woman (Jn 4:4-42)

- Many similarities are noticed between the demoniac's story and the story of the Samaritan Woman.

- Much to the Samaritan Woman's surprise, Jesus (a male and a Jew) takes initiative to reach out to her (a woman and a Samaritan and an outcast even among her own people). Jesus cut across the prejudices and historical barriers to initiate a

74

relationship with her as an individual person having her own specific cultural and personal background.

- The more she talks with him, the more she awakens to some new realizations about the truth of herself and what she's searching for in her life.

- Touched by what she's experiencing as Good News, she puts down her water jar and hurries back to the town to tell the people: "Come and see a man who has told me everything I ever did. . . . I wonder if he is the Christ. . . ." She invites them to come and meet a person, the person of Jesus, who has had an effect on her life.

- The fire in the testimony she gave and the noticeable change within her caused people to wonder and seek this person, Jesus.

- More and more people began to believe. As members of a community, they influenced each other's ability to believe.

- All there come to a deeper belief now because of the personal relationship they develop with Jesus and with each other. Their faith becomes rooted not just in the woman's or anyone else's experience, but in their own individual experience of Jesus.

C. Both Accounts Show

- All people are called to evangelization, even those who seem most "unlikely."

- Evangelization flows out of a consciousness of what God has done for the person who is evangelizing and a burning desire to have others experience this God, too, in their own personal lives.

- The evangelist is an agent for Jesus, preparing the way and representing him in places he is yet unable to enter.

- The evangelist is a person freed by Jesus; one who has entered into a relationship with Jesus that he/she has found freeing and now wants to spread that Good News.

- Evangelists are very ordinary people, witnessing among ordinary persons who live and work around them, sharing with them their own story of coming to a new experience of joy and freedom. Neighbors seem amazed, yet drawn, by this sharing which is so convincing.

II. Evangelii Nuntiandi *and Other Documents as Basis*

A. "It is the whole Church (all the baptized) that receives the mission to evangelize, and the work of each individual member is important for the whole" (no. 15).

B. "Lay people, whose particular vocation places them in the midst of the world and in charge of the most varied temporal tasks, must for this very reason exercise a very special form of evangelization" (no. 70). "One cannot fail to stress the evangelizing action of the family in the evangelizing apostolate of the laity" (no. 71).

C. "We must continue our task to evangelization with courage and trust, even if the times are more difficult than in the past" (Pope John Paul II, *Address to the Pontifical Mission Aid Societies*, May 8, 1987).

D. "Evangelization is the work of all the members of the Church: bishops, theologians, priests, religious, and laity, both adult and youth" (Pope John Paul II, *Address to the Bishops of Belgium*, April 24, 1987).

E. U.S. Catholic bishops' recent documents addressing the laity as agents of evangelization:

- *Called and Gifted: The American Catholic Laity*, National Conference of Catholic Bishops, 1980;

- *The Hispanic Presence: Challenge and Commitment*, NCCB, 1983;

- *National Pastoral Plan for Hispanic Ministry*, NCCB, 1987;

- *What We Have Seen and Heard*, a Pastoral Letter on Evangelization from the Black Bishops of the United States, 1984;

- *A Family Perspective in Church and Society*, NCCB, 1988.

III. *The American Cultural, Political, and Religious Reality: A Challenge to Lay Evangelizers*

A. In the daily civic life of American Catholics, democracy is their way of life where they have a voice, where they are expected to be active participants in promoting and serving that form of life.

   American Catholics find it difficult to live this type of life in civil society, which is quite different from our hierarchical mode of life, which for a long time expected Catholics to limit their involvement to paying and praying only.

B. Roman Catholics live side by side with Christians of other denominations. They see their non-Catholic brothers and sisters participating as preachers almost from the moment they are baptized. But also see them active in so many other ways. They have been a big source of challenge to our Catholic people. Many of them have gotten involved in the Catholic Church because of the example they have seen in these other brothers and sisters.

IV. *Need for the Evangelization because of the U.S. Reality*

A. Society in General

   A list of some characteristics of the United States, its culture and practices, which could have an effect upon evangelization efforts by the Catholic Church in America. This listing is by no means exhaustive, yet it represents some very prevalent trends in U.S. society.

   1. Narcissism/individualism/emphasis on individual:

      • emphasis on "doing own thing"; "don't need anyone else"; "I have no impact on anyone else"; "nothing wrong with me";

- from a nation of immigrants, multicultural with great diversity, wanting not only independence as individuals, but expression as a culture, a "people";
- perhaps "best" or most dramatically experienced in political corruption; nothing will hinder the attainment of what's best for "me."

2. Consumerism.

3. Accelerated change.

4. Disintegration of marriage and family life:
   - large divorce rate;
   - single-parent families (many times in poverty);
   - remarriage;
   - cohabitation.

5. Mobility, lack of roots.

6. Ecumenical relationships:
   - statistics show 28 percent of Catholics in their 20s are in ecumenical marriage; 21 percent in their 30s; 18 percent in their 40s; 14 percent in their 50s or older—evangelization?

7. Lack of Christian values as the center for individual/family:
   - commitment to Christian family values.

8. The Church has not reached out:
   - historically, possibly didn't need to, because people were in need of the Church, they came to the Church.

9. Growth of sects:
   - especially those with fundamentalistic orientation.

10. Lack of emphasis on the dignity of life.

B. The Institutional Church

1. Only 44 percent of youth attend Mass every Sunday and of those who do, only 24 percent would go if their parents didn't force them ("The Young and Restless," James Breig, *U.S. Catholic*, December 1988, p. 10). The percentage of 44

percent, while lower, reflects what is happening in the *adult* Catholic population with *half* of adult Catholics not attending Mass regularly.

2. The 1987 Gallup Poll "On Youth Religious Attitudes" indicated that 71 percent of the youth surveyed say they pray, but only 40 percent expressed any involvement in institutional programs; yet 70 percent said they valued religious affiliation. These figures reflect the observations of Catholic diocesan directors of youth in the publication *Youth Ministry in the United States*: "youth want to participate in the life of the Church but feel distant and not welcomed as members of the Church."

3. The Church in the United States still struggles with an organizational model of evangelization versus a ministerial model. The former, while effective to a degree, tends to compartmentalize rather than unify. As a result, our evangelization efforts lack a common vision and a unified plan of implementation both on a parish level and on a diocesan level. Competition, not cooperation, characterizes many efforts to bring the Gospel to the churched and unchurched in many parishes.

4. The Catholic experience in the United States was one of an immigrant Church needing to protect itself against a society that was predominantly Anglo and Protestant. Because we have been more self-preserving than outward looking, we have struggled with the reaching out needed to be evangelizers.

5. Our theology prior to Vatican II did not prepare us to reach out. Clergy were the Church, and the laity participated in the mission of the clergy. As a result, we as Church are immature in our preparation to evangelize.

6. The call for laity to live out their baptismal commitment has motivated many to seek formation and training for ministry.

7. The U.S. Church has been successful in passing on the dogma (in teaching religion) but weaker in communicating faith which is conscious, living, and active—one which is countercultural and changes institutions and society.

8. Examples of success stories in outreach and evangelization from the other churches (e.g., Mormons, Jehovah's Witnesses, Baptists).

V. Present Reality—Laity as Agents of Evangelization

To respond to the above needs of people, our own active Catholics need to be helped to fall more in love with Jesus, to be converted to him, to make him central to their lives, to imitate him, and to share their experiences of him with others.

This is happening—as with the demoniac who was cured; as with the Samaritan Woman and many others. Our people today are experiencing the Lord and then going to their families, to their communities and telling others "what wonders the Lord in his mercy has done for them." Upon hearing, they, too, believe and praise the Lord.

Responding to the Present Reality

The Church in the United States is responding through the following manner:

- Half of the population of U.S. Catholics do attend church.

- Family evangelization from a systems perspective is the focus of evangelization in today's Church—efforts at catechizing the family.

- Formation of basic Christian communities—efforts at developing "house churches" in larger parishes.

- National thrust at adult education, making it the center of the Church's mission rather than at the periphery—evident in the following:

  • Bible study groups: Little Rock Program;

  • Adult Bible Interdependent Learning;

  • Share the Word;

  • Prayer groups;

  • Charismatic groups sharing prayer;

  • Rosary groups;

- Scripture reflection groups;
- Lay institutes for formation have flourished;
- Large percentage of lay people receiving theological formation in institutes.

- Movements:
  - Cursillo;
  - Engaged and Marriage Encounters;
  - Focolare;
  - Christian Life Movement/Christian Family Movement;
  - Better World Movements in areas;
  - Parish Renewals, Missions, RENEW;
  - Rite of Christian Initiation of Adults;
  - Perpetual Adoration in churches.

- Retreat Movements:
  - Laity;
  - ACTS (Adoration-Community-Thanksgiving-Service).

- Lay Liturgical Renewal and Formation:
  - Lectors;
  - Eucharistic ministers;
  - Music ministers;
  - Greeters;
  - Ushers;
  - Sacramental preparation by lay people in parishes.

- Lay Life-Care Ministries:
  - Outreach to the sick in nursing homes, hospitals, housebound.

- Stephen's Ministries—interfaith outreach program to "hurting" persons in parishes.

- Lay Peer-Support Groups:
  - Widowed
  - Divorced

- Singles.
- Lay Preachers as Evangelizers.
- Youth Peer-Ministry Outreach:
  - Teens Encounter Christ;
  - National Evangelization Teams;
  - Search for Christian Maturity;
  - Catholic Charismatic Youth Movement.
- Catholic Schools (now staffed in the majority by lay people) in the United States have been and are centers of evangelization.
- Lay Catechists in Parish Catechetical Programs.
- Collaborative Ministries:
  - Pastoral associates in parishes;
  - Pastoral administrators in parishes.
- Paulist Evangelization Center.
- Participation of the laity in the consultation processes requested by the American bishops has led to a heightened critical consciousness in the following areas:
  - National Catechetical Directory (catechesis);
  - War And peace (pastoral);
  - Economy (pastoral);
  - Women's issues (pastoral draft).
- Laity on finance councils responsible for stewardship within the Church (both parish and diocesan).
- Laity as part of parish and diocesan pastoral councils.
- Mission Texas Project scheduled for 1990—result of the pope's visit to the United States in 1987.

The Family
(Pastoral Ministry to the Family, the Indissolubility of Marriage, Marriage Cases Handled in the Local Tribunal)

Edouard Cardinal Gagnon

Marriage and the family represent a field of pastoral concern where it is most difficult for bishops to exercise this teaching mission freely and with immediate and visible success. The authentic teaching of the Church has usually to go against what is commonly promoted in the secularist schools and mass media, and is often misunderstood or misrepresented inside the Church itself. Marriage and family questions permeate every sphere of pastoral activity, and it is surely impossible for any superior to know and eventually to correct every error or imprudence that can be made for diverse motives and at diverse levels.

It is indeed cumbersome and irritating at times to hear families complain about what is being taught to their children, about the way they are dealt with and the values they feel are in danger; but listening to them might be the only way we have to know what is happening at the grass roots of our Catholic communities and institutions. Our ordinary people, the ones who care about their family life, have not been trained in the ways of making representations to us with all the due nuances and distinctions. We have to be patient with them. Is it not a sign of the vitality of a Church when simple people manifest their worries and their attachment to certain well-proven expressions of their faith and religious practice? In too many places they are just resigned or indifferent.

A. *Encouraging Signs*

It is not to me to summarize the very positive information which reaches our pontifical council on the pastoral activities of the U.S. hierarchy. I would like though to point out certain achievements which have been perceived by pastoral workers in other countries as an encouragement in their efforts to defend and promote family values. (What happens in your country always has an influence, especially in the developing countries, but also in Europe.)

1. Abortion

Entrusted with the task of following and sustaining the pro-life movement, our council has witnessed with great interest the progress which the courageous work of laity and clergy since the *Roe vs. Wade* decision has realized in forming consciences and changing mentalities. When endeavoring to obtain laws which respect the Creator's plan and the genuine purpose of society, the American Church has not yet obtained everything it would desire, but it has demonstrated that even adverse public events can become a providential occasion for that essential part of evangelization which is to defend the most fundamental right of the human person.

By explaining the reasons and the consequences of the right to life, you have made many to understand what is expressed in the *Charter of the Rights of the Family*: "Economic aid for the advancement of peoples must not be conditioned on acceptance of programs of contraception, sterilization, or abortion. . . . To attempt in any way to limit the freedom of couples in deciding about their children constitutes a grave offense against human dignity and justice."

The presence of three cardinals at the last "March for Life" in Washington has given a boost to people not only in the United States but all over the world.

The bishops in charge of the family apostolate for bishops' conferences in more than 50 countries, at the meeting held in this hall in November, have begged their brother bishops of politically powerful nations to protect them from the new form of colonialism which anti-life programs constitute. They are sure you can do something to defend them.

2. Pornography

Another domain in which bishops of other countries count on your leadership is that of reacting against the diffusion of pornography. I know you are trying to work with all people of good will in defending youth and adults alike against the danger to their personhood coming from pornography and the potent industries behind it. I would suggest that we do something too about another and more subtle pornography, that is, the degrading of moral values vehicled by cinema and TV shows which pretend to depict normal American life. At a U.N. meeting, a sociologist defined the developed and underdeveloped nations as those who looked at or could not look at the "Dallas" TV series.

CBS News this week showed how a young Illinois mother has managed by herself to get Procter and Gamble and other big advertisers to stop sponsoring a particularly offensive program, which rendered more difficult her educating her children. We feel our fellow citizens are adult enough to resist such poisonous food. But the pastors of other worlds would like us to reflect on how what we export can affect the conscience of their people.

3. Natural Family Planning

The recent development of national episcopal coordination for NFP will be a great help for so many who have worked in the field for years, often in the midst of indifference for their apostolic commitment and of harsh opposition to *Humanae Vitae*. The success they have obtained is due not only to their faith, but also to their spirit of initiative and inventiveness. This has caused a certain divisiveness between schools, which we should try to remedy but patiently, and in the respect of a certain plurality of approach. A problem has emerged about which we have to be vigilant. That of combining NFP with methods of artificial contraception, at times because the International Planned Parenthood Federation or similar groups try to infiltrate Catholic associations and corrupt and pirate NFP methods.

4. Education for Chastity

The Pontifical Council for the Family, then under the direction of Cardinal Knox, received as one of its first missions that of studying the implications the document *Education in Human Sexuality*

for Christians: Guidelines for Discussion and Planning could have
on preparing young people for a successful married life and helping them to preserve chastity before marriage.

We are happy to see that a revision of the guidelines has been
undertaken under the direction of a bishops' commission and that
it will not be just a superficial one, but will take its distance from
the philosophical principles which, as was underlined at the beginning of this meeting, have conditioned the pedagogical formation
of many educators.

We hope such a revision will bring about the revision of other
educational material based on the guidelines.

5. Family Perspective

Your publication of a manual for pastoral leaders titled *A Family Perspective in Church and Society* is a valid expression of what
the Synod on the Family wanted to be the full dimension of the
ministry to families and of families. We have been happy to recommend it to bishops wishing to give a better structured form to their
pastoral care of the family.

B. Points of Concern

Without departing from a fundamental optimism about the
Church in the United States, I think I must signal some matters
on which we should work together better to ensure the interest of
the family.

1. Indissolubility of Marriage and Marriage Tribunals

You know what fields of pastoral reflection and action have been
entrusted to the Council for the Family. The first matter I want to
mention is one where we share a common concern with the tribunal
of the Roman Rota. The prevalent divorce mentality has rendered
the role of marriage tribunals most essential and at the same time
most complex.

We teach by word of mouth, but even more by what we do. If
young people or married couples going through the unavoidable
crisis of conjugal life feel that it is easy to get a declaration of nullity, faith in the possibility of permanent love and commitment will

decrease ever more. We know you are worried about the problems you are confronted with because of the lack of personnel for the tribunals and the huge number of broken marriages. Two things, I believe, need special attention.

The first one is the choice of the personnel. When I was in Alberta, after some surprising sentences had been referred to our bishops' planning sessions, we found that our officialis, who had been a teacher of theology, did not believe in the indissolubility of marriage. Women religious can be very helpful in dealing with marriage cases, but we have to be careful that their tender hearts do not play tricks on them.

A second thing which is important is making sure that both parties are equally listened to before a sentence is pronounced. It happens that one hears from the tribunal after his or her marriage has been declared invalid.

2. Marriage Preparation and Doctrine

Linked with the precedent question is that of preparation for marriage. Serious surveys have made you verify the fact that all dioceses have well-structured programs. But nobody will be surprised if we say that the content of these can easily reflect the theological trends already mentioned here.

From our observation point at the council, I think we should not be pessimistic about the possibility of reversing trends and chang ing the climate of hostility which has been prevalent against the magisterium's doctrine on conjugal morality. The congress at Princeton last summer for the 20th anniversary of *Humanae Vitae*, with scholars of very diverse backgrounds, the coming of age of a new generation of moralists, together with a wider recognition of the social and moral disaster a contraceptive mentality can lead to, are not motives for complacency but are positive indicators.

But an equivocal concept of the role of conscience can linger in pastoral practice even after more orthodox theologians have been brought into our major seminaries and universities. I admire the wisdom of some bishops who have invited doctrinally competent and experienced spiritual directors to clarify with their priests the notions they need to guide their faithful out of the present confusion. The number of good young couples who look for sound spiritual guidance is much greater than we would think.

I would also submit, with humility, that a bishop would not be losing his time if he personally reviewed the diocesan programs and literature pertaining to marriage preparation. He could then see if they have been revised to reflect what the bishops have proposed at the 1980 Synod and the Holy Father has vividly summarized in *Familiaris Consortio*. Such a revision would surely stress the peculiarity and dynamism of the sacrament of matrimony and the power of sacramental grace, which makes the observance of God's law possible.

A new challenge is offered to the Church by the efforts of Planned Parenthood to set up school-based clinics for abortion referral and contraception. A way to oppose this menace in all dioceses would be to develop a united policy and practice on a national level. Planned Parenthood programs of sex education in no way resolve the problem of teen-age pregnancies, but rather increase it by encouraging promiscuity. The statistical fact surprisingly turned up in one of their own surveys.

I have often come upon parish bulletins referring people to IPPF centers or commending their initiatives. Maybe something could be done to inform priests and other parish workers about such agencies.

3. Other Questions

I have already exceeded my time, but I would end by enumerating some of the concerns we share with you.

a) One is the question of *sterilization* in Catholic hospitals and, in a more general way, among Catholic people. Some faithful active in family life education in conformity with church teaching are surprised often to hear that men who are known to have been sterilized are ordained as permanent deacons.

b) Another question is the spreading of *euthanasia*. The young lady who addressed many of you at a conference in Texas recently is probably the best informed person in the world about the word engineering that leads to idea engineering and could ultimately lead to legalization of euthanasia, as it has done for abortion.

c) A further question is that of the *ministry to the divorced and remarried*. Some forms of such ministry, ignoring the principles set in *Familiaris Consortio*, have degenerated into dating services for divorced Catholics who are not free to marry. I know that their promoters are personages who cannot easily be brought under episcopal control. Maybe some guidelines coming from your conference could help priests and faithful in their discernment.

d) *Homosexuality.* At a theological congress after Vatican II and before *Humanae Vitae*, a prominent woman professor of philosophy at Oxford said that, if we accepted sex without children through contraception, we would be led to accept homosexuality as a way of life.

e) *Feminism.* It is evident that ideological feminism has a deleterious influence on the family. But, conversely, the best way to counter its influence will be to care more about the family and make everyone in it more conscious of his or her vocation "to serve and not to be served," as Christ has taught us. Much is being said here about feminism. I would just like to remark that when we work, as we should, for the promotion of women, we should be careful in choosing the persons we work with. I know a country where the woman who led the team that went around the dioceses to present a bishops' working paper on the status of women in the Church was a well known dissenter from *Humanae Vitae* and a proponent of freedom of choice for abortion.

Intervention

Achille Cardinal Silvestrini

In this brief intervention, it is my intention as prefect of the Supreme Tribunal of the Apostolic Signatura to offer some general reflections on the matter of marriage nullity cases in the United States. First of all, the Apostolic Signatura readily acknowledges and appreciates the great effort made in the United States to give the faithful the possibility of obtaining, within a reasonable time, the declaration of nullity of a marriage which really is null, in order then to exercise their fundamental right to contract a true marriage. The Apostolic Signatura has, however, some areas of difficulty. I deem it opportune to point these out briefly in the context of the present sincere and frank dialogue.

Using data taken from the Church's *Statistical Yearbook for 1985*, the latest edition, we find that 37,538 ordinary process decisions were given in first instance in the United States; of these 36,180 were affirmative and 1,358 were negative. In the same year, a total of 48,453 decisions were given worldwide; of these 45,632 were affirmative and 2,821 were negative (*Annuarium Statisticum Ecclesiae*, pp. 381-387). When the comparison is made with other no less advanced countries with good functioning tribunals, the large number of declarations of nullity in the United States—more than 36,000—is a source of surprise. This number certainly represents in part also those marriages contracted between non-Catholics. There remain, nonetheless, very many marriages declared null which were contracted by Catholics. This fact of itself constitutes a serious problem for the pastoral care of marriage, namely, what must be done to prevent so many marriages which end in nullity in the Church in the United States?

From the many recourses which come to the Apostolic Signatura one may deduce that various tribunals in the United States have introduced their own method, not fully in conformity with the *Code of Canon Law*, in instructing marriage cases. For example, the frequent use of so-called affidavits in taking depositions and written testimony. It is clear that the adequate examination of so many cases poses serious problems. But it is also obvious that a marriage nullity case demands a particularly diligent investigation: one is dealing with the declaration of nullity of the sacred bond of marriage.

As is true in some other countries also, there is a very high percentage of declarations of nullity on the grounds of so-called psychic incapacity (c. 1095: 2,3). The Apostolic Signatura wonders whether there prevails confusion:

- between maturity understood in the psychological sense and in the canonical sense of the term;
- between authentic incapacity and difficulty in assuming the essential obligations of marriage;
- between valid marriage and happy marriage.

According to many modern psychologists, those persons who do not reach true psychological maturity are not few. The institution of marriage, however, cannot be considered as reserved just to a chosen few; canonical maturity requires only that minimum of intention and will which is necessary to validly contract marriage. It is to be hoped that valid marriages are also happy ones; but it must be made very clear that only true incapacity to assume the obligations of marriage and not just difficulties encountered by the parties causes nullity of marriage from the outset. It is necessary that tribunals keep in mind the doctrine proposed in this regard by the supreme pontiff in his allocutions to the Roman Rota on February 5, 1987, and January 25, 1988.

Finally, the Apostolic Signatura has encountered in various cases from the United States—and also from some other countries—grave violations of the right of defense. It seems that this occurs in order to avoid eventual recourse to civil litigation. One cannot understand, in a democratic nation in which the principle of the separation of church and state prevails, that there could be a *de facto* submission of ecclesiastical to civil jurisdiction. Whatever the case, it seems opportune to reiterate that violation of the right of defense is not conceivable in the Church today and can never be an effective means of protecting oneself from eventual recourse to a civil state.

I have put forward with sincerity and frankness certain anxieties of the Apostolic Signatura, which I submit for the bishops' reflection. The bishops, even more than the officials who make up the tribunals, are responsible for the administration of justice. It is in no way my intention to pass over the good work which is being done. I wish only to ask that vigilance be employed so that it be done even better.

Archbishop John Quinn

On the morning of September 18, 1987, our Holy Father, Pope John Paul II, addressed 3,000 lay men and women from all parts of the United States in St. Mary's Cathedral in San Francisco. He said, "Of supreme importance in the mission of the Church is the role that the laity fulfill in the Christian family. This role is above all a service of love and a service of life."

Because they are of supreme importance in the mission of the Church, marriage and the family similarly form a supremely important part of the content of evangelization. The heart of the Church's evangelization on marriage and the family is the divinely revealed truth that marriage is the sacrament of the union of Christ and the Church. For this reason, the ecclesiological dimensions of marriage are an important part of the mission of evangelization. The sacrament of the union of Christ and the Church, Christian marriage, is indissoluble. It is also because of this ecclesiological dimension of marriage that the family is called "the domestic church," as *Familiaris Consortio* so clearly emphasizes. As such, the family itself is an instrument of evangelization and is a fundamental source for the transmission of both religion and civilization. It is through the family that each successive generation first comes to know the saving message of Christ and the Church. And it is through the family that the values and principles of the Christian moral life are first communicated. The family also fulfills the mission of evangelization in that it is the soil in which the seed of priestly and religious vocations germinate.

I. Challenges to Evangelization

Gaudium et Spes taught the Church to scrutinize the signs of the times in the light of the Gospel. In the brief time allotted to me here I cannot, of course, touch on everything important. But I would at least highlight some of the signs of the times which we experience in the United States and how they affect marriage and family life.

As the Holy Father observed in his San Francisco address, ". . . [W]e must recognize the difficult situation of so many people with regard to family living. There are many with special burdens of one kind or another." Among the specific examples mentioned by

93

the Holy Father are single-parent families and those who have no natural families: the elderly and the widowed, and separated and divorced Catholics. He also mentions secularism, relativism, and consumerism. I would also note that the council sees pluralism as a worldwide phenomenon having repercussions on all facets of life, including the religious.

And so, among the many challenges which our society offers to the Church's mission of evangelization on marriage and the family, I would mention the following:

1. *The shift of emphasis from the economic and social conception of marriage to the personalist conception of marriage.* This means that relationships within marriage and the family are viewed as important in themselves and not merely for the function they afford society. There is no question that this shift has enriched family life in the United States by emphasizing the teaching of *Gaudium et Spes* that married life should be characterized by friendship and deep mutual love between husband and wife. At the same time, an exaggerated and unrealistic overemphasis on the personalist conception of marriage has led, in the minds of many, to a disregard for the institutional dimensions of marriage and to the belief that marriage must fulfill all of an individual's needs and dreams if it is to make any legitimate claims on him. Such a distorted personalism does not testify to the self-sacrificial and indissoluble dimensions of married life nor to the common-sense realism that no human relationship is capable of meeting every need and desire.

2. *Marriage as relegated to the private sphere.* Recent studies (e.g., *Habits of the Heart*) indicate that the family "is no longer an integral part of a larger moral ecology tying the individual to community, church, and nation. The family is the core of the private sphere, whose aim is not to link individuals to the public world, but to avoid it as far as possible."

This tendency toward privatization, of course, poses a fundamental challenge to the ecclesial character of marriage and the family. If the prevailing view relegates the family to the private sphere, dissociated from the community and the church, then what meaning can those affected by this mentality find in the description of the family as *ecclesia domestica*? The family is being further assailed by the privatizing movement in areas where there are growing efforts to legalize "marriages" between persons of the same sex.

3. *The media. Gaudium et Spes*, speaking of the signs of the times, noted that "new and more efficient media of social communication are contributing to the knowledge of events. By setting off chain reactions, they are giving the swiftest and widest possible circulation to styles of thought and feeling." Thus, while the media have brought to the people of the United States unparalleled access to information about our world, the picture which the media present is often shaped by philosophical presuppositions which serve to undercut the stability and role of marriage and the family. For example, the media's commitment to "religious neutrality" has all too often led to a purely secular view of the world which, consequently, ignores the sacred dimensions of marriage, family, and social life. The commitment to "value neutrality" has led the media to present marriage and family as merely one life style among many competing life styles in society rather than as the foundation for social life and education. And the media's desire not to alienate too many of its watchers and readers has all too often led to surface coverage of divisive issues rather than to the type of probing and substantive public debate which would reveal, for instance, the true evil and danger of abortion and of some reproductive technologies. Also, the media, through advertising as well as through its general offerings—editorial, dramatic, news reporting, etc.—reflect and contribute to the trivialized view that sexuality is merely an instrument for personal gratification rather than a gift with profound unitive and creative dimensions.

4. *The economic situation of increasing numbers of Americans, more and more of whom are slipping below the poverty line or moving closer and closer to it.* This has led to the increased need for both parents in a family to work and has consequent undesirable effects on children in many instances and exerts great pressures on the marriage itself. Another phenomenon inimical to family life is the widening number of families who are homeless. Increasingly large numbers of children, even in our largest and greatest cities, are living below the poverty level; and this, of course, has implications for their emotional and human growth as well as for their ability to improve their lot in the future, since this kind of poverty makes it likely that they will never acquire sufficient education to improve or to participate in a meaningful and positive way in society. In the United States we are witnessing the new phenomenon of people who want to work and who are able to work being literally trapped in poverty. There is no way out. There

are fewer and fewer jobs for the unskilled and the untrained. And very often the jobs they can find yield a salary insufficient to support a family.

5. *The widespread use of drugs and the abuse of alcohol.* The worldwide phenomenon of drug and alcohol abuse was not clearly foreseen by the council, but it must now be numbered among the signs of the times. The use of drugs requires large sums of money and is often linked with violent crime. Both drugs and the excessive use of alcohol also often affect the personality of the user and have consequent effects on the marriage relationship and on the ability of parents to relate to, to be concerned about, and to care properly for their children. It is widely known and documented that alcohol abuse has profound and far-reaching effects on both children and the marriage relationship.

6. *Pluralism and mobility.* In addition to the widespread religious and philosophical pluralism characteristic of the United States, I must also note the ethnic and cultural pluralism within the Church. Some groups within the Church have a very strong family life, notably Hispanics and Filipinos, while the average American Catholic family has been more vulnerable to the societal attacks on family life and marriage. There seems to be a closer and more stable family life in rural areas generally, in contrast with urban areas. There is also, however, high mobility in the population in the United States. And this, in turn, means that one part of a family living, for example, on the East Coast may move 3,000 miles away to California and thus be separated from other members of the family. This is a very common phenomenon which, of course, in many instances places stress on the family.

Many more signs of the times which exert stress on the family could be mentioned. But these serve as some indication of the difficulties which the Church encounters from society in its effort to fulfill its mission of evangelization concerning marriage and the family.

II. The Church's Response

In light of these considerations, two questions emerge. What attitude should the Church have toward these difficulties? And what is the Church in the United States doing in the face of these challenges to fulfill its mission of evangelization concerning marriage and the family?

First of all, it must never be forgotten that if the Church did nothing else but faithfully celebrate the Eucharist and proclaim the Word of God, she would be offering an indispensable service to humanity. And so no matter what else the Church does or does not do in an effort to remedy the specific evils of a given age, she is always faithfully carrying out the fundamental mission given to her. The Church often experiences what the Lord himself experienced: His efforts at evangelization, even with the apostles themselves, were not uniformly effective, and as we read in the Gospels, his mission was ultimately ridiculed and rejected by the larger society of his time. The Church, then, must walk in the light of the Lord's saying, "The servant is not greater than the master. . . . They will pay as much attention to your words as they pay to mine." Success cannot be the criterion or the condition of evangelization. The criterion and condition of evangelization must be fidelity to the mission. And so the attitude of the Church in the face of these immense challenges must be one of unshakable hope based on the conviction that Christ crucified in weakness and risen in power is always at work even in the seemingly most hopeless situation, and despite what it may seem, we are always being "transformed from glory into glory."

Nevertheless, in the power of the Eucharist and the Word of God, the Church is making serious and effective efforts to confront these challenges and fulfill its mission of evangelization. For example, of the 177 dioceses in the United States, 144 have family life offices to promote the good of families and to assist them in various ways.

An increasing number of dioceses have marriage preparation programs in which all couples desiring to marry participate. These programs not infrequently last at least six months and include instruction on the sacramentality of marriage, the responsibilities of marriage and childbearing, the spirituality of marriage, and the pursuit of holiness through marriage. They also offer various practical helps for dealing with the problems and challenges which married life and fidelity to the Church's teaching may involve. The National Conference of Catholic Bishops has recently approved the publication of a manual intended to aid in marriage preparation and to standardize the preparation in light of the vast size of our country and the high mobility of the population.

A significant aspect of the marriage preparation programs which underlines the ecclesial dimension of marriage is the wide involvement of married couples in carrying out the programs themselves. This ecclesial role of married couples helping others to prepare for marriage is a concrete manifestation of the connection of marriage and the family to the Church and to the larger society.

Many of these programs are parish-based. This also promotes the ecclesial connection between the family and the believing, worshiping community. These parochial programs often involve engaged couples meeting in the homes of married couples thereby indicating the connection between the home and the parish community founded on the sacrament of marriage.

Also, more than 3 million couples have made the Marriage Encounter weekend retreat since 1970. Many of these couples have found that this experience has strengthened their marriage and has made them more faithful to the Church and her sacramental life. There are more than 20,000 married couples across the country who work in giving these retreat weekends to other married couples. For marriages in which the couple is experiencing difficulties, many dioceses provide counseling and spiritual direction to assist them. New programs, such as Retrouvaille, are emerging precisely to assist troubled marriages.

Many dioceses have established a policy requiring parents to take part in a series of instruction and preparation sessions before the baptism of their children. Parents are also required in many dioceses to take part with their children in their preparation for holy communion and confession and in their preparation for confirmation.

The parishes of the United States are providing both a religious and a social context which nourishes family life and the Christian understanding of marriage. By uniting families in the Eucharist and the sacramental life of the Church, our parishes reinforce the relationship of parents and children with Christ and the Church and encourage families to see God as an intimate and indispensable part of their family life. That this is effective seems to be demonstrated by the fact that in the United States some 54 percent of Catholics attend Mass each Sunday, while 72 percent attend Mass at least once each month.

By educating children in the message of the Gospel, our parishes assist parents in the most important evangelical work of their married life: to transmit the faith of the Church to their children. By providing a place where families can socialize together with others who share their commitment to the person and message of Christ, the parishes of the United States help to compensate for the rootlessness and lack of social and religious support that are inherent in our society with its secularistic stance and high mobility. And by emphasizing that family life is part of the larger life of the Church, our parishes counter the privatizing trends of marriage and family life in America.

It should be noted also that the Church in the United States has taken very significant steps to address some of the structural causes of the problems in marriage and family life in our country. For instance, the bishops have been forthright in addressing the social and economic issues which underlie some of these problems such as poverty, homelessness, abortion, and drug abuse. The bishops have done this through national pastoral letters, through testimony before Congress, through programs under the auspices of diocesan Catholic Charities, social justice commissions, and family life offices.

Living in a pluralistic society where divorce is commonly accepted, the Catholic Church often stands alone in its teaching on the indissolubility of marriage. The defense of marriage is evident in our diocesan tribunals. Many non-Catholics, in the desire to be received into communion with the Church or to marry a Catholic, petition our tribunals to examine the nullity of their marriages which have been previously dissolved by a civil tribunal. The time, expense, and personnel given to the work of our tribunals give a clear message to these non-Catholics that the Church takes the indissolubility of marriage very seriously. The pastoral application of the Church's canonical procedures, done in justice, charity, and fidelity to truth, is a clear moment of evangelization on marriage. When done with pastoral sensitivity, the work of our tribunals can be a manifestation of the Church's concern for the individual person as well as an invitation to understand more fully the Church's rich teaching on marriage.

As we conclude this very limited reflection on this panorama of sin and grace in the midst of which the Church in the United States fulfills its mission, it is good to call to mind the words of St. Ambrose: "The Church of the Lord is built upon the rock of the apostles among so many dangers in the world; it therefore remains unmoved. The Church's foundation is unshakable and firm against the assaults of the raging sea. Waves lash at the Church but do not shatter it. Although the elements of this world constantly beat upon the Church with crashing sounds, the Church possesses the safest harbor of salvation for all in distress."

The Christian Education of the Young

William Cardinal Baum

The topic for discussion at this session is a vast one; I will limit my remarks to that part of the Christian education of youth which takes place within a school and, except for a brief mention of other educational institutions at the end, I will speak only about education within *Catholic* schools, colleges, and universities. In keeping with the purposes of these meetings, the presentation will focus especially on those concerns which the American bishops have raised in their *Ad Limina* visits and in their quinquennial reports, along with concerns expressed in similar documents which have been received in the Congregation.

For the sake of clarity, I would like to speak first about Catholic primary and secondary schools and then separately about Catholic colleges and universities.

Primary and Secondary Schools

The commitment of the Church in the United States to a well-developed network of Catholic primary and secondary schools began at the time of the Baltimore Councils, and that same commitment continues to the present day, these schools have provided Catholic formation for generations of youth and have been one of the major reasons for the vitality of the Church in America. At the same time, the fulfillment of that commitment has called for a tremendous amount of dedication and sacrifice on the part of bishops, priests, religious, and laity, and the entire Church in America deserves thanks and praise for the great good that has been achieved. The concern that is expressed today is how to maintain and improve these schools in the light of the current sociocultural context and in the face of rather serious difficulties.

101

One of the primary difficulties is financial. These schools, maintained without government subsidy, have always called for financial sacrifice on the part of parents, parishes, and dioceses. Today, in an age of increasing professionalism, the cost of education keeps on rising dramatically while at the same time, the numbers of religious and priests who have traditionally staffed the schools with very little financial remuneration continue to decrease. The problem is serious, and it exists in every diocese, but the problem is most severe in those parishes located in the poorer sections of large metropolitan centers, where the need to educate is the greatest but the resources for providing this education are the most scarce.

There is no easy solution to the problem of finances, and it is not a problem that is going to disappear in the near future. I can only urge you, with your fellow bishops: first, to continue seeking sources of private funding, whether through endowments or through other means; and second, to continue, as forcefully as you can, to press for public recognition and support of Catholic schools as a matter of justice. The need for these schools is as great today as it has ever been, and I want you to know that your efforts have the support of the Holy See. Catholic education at the primary and secondary levels forms the young men and women who will enter society in all walks of life; it is a source of vocations to the priesthood and religious life, and often it is the training ground for those who provide leadership in parishes and dioceses. There is a special need to maintain the schools in poorer areas and to open all Catholic schools to the disadvantaged, including Blacks, Hispanics, Asian refugees, and other minority groups.

The question of finances, while it is very real, must not command our attention to such an extent that we are not sufficiently attentive to other concerns—all of which have to do with providing that total human, moral, and spiritual formation in Catholic schools which is the reason for their existence. I will mention only a few of the more significant ones.

1. *The proper religious formation of their children is a concern of many parents.* As you know, this formation is accomplished through the entire life of the school, in the classroom and outside of it. But the concern expressed often has to do with the explicitly religious formation given through catechetical instruction and religious studies. We must make sure that Catholic young people are taught the basic truths of the Catholic faith, both doctrinal and

moral; that they grow in an appreciation of the sacraments; and that they are made conscious of what it means to be members of the Catholic Church. Ensuring that an adequate religious formation is available to Catholic young people, especially in Catholic schools, is a major responsibility of every bishop; certainly the forthcoming Universal Catechism—or Compendium of Catholic Doctrine—which will be normative for all catechesis, will be an indispensable aid in the fulfillment of this responsibility.

2. *The need for an adequate religious formation of the students reinforces the need already felt for an improved religious formation of the teachers who are educating these students.* Today most of these teachers are lay men and women; their religious formation cannot be taken for granted. I know that there are already many programs designed to provide religious formation for teachers, but I would urge you to give their concern greater attention. The lay teachers in our Catholic schools are, in general, filled with dedication and good will, but they must also have the formation they need in order to be the models and the source of the religious formation of our young people.

3. Finally, let me very briefly mention *the need for greater involvement of parents in the life of the school and in the education of their children.* Their involvement can assist in their own human and religious formation and can be a great help in the formation of the young people.

Colleges and Universities

The concerns at the level of Catholic colleges and universities are similar to those of the schools and at the same time are distinct.

1. *Religious formation at the post-secondary level ought to be part of the maturing process through which a personal faith commitment is integrated into one's life and work.* Unfortunately, more and more students are entering college today without an adequate knowledge of the basic truths of the Catholic faith, and we must find ways to remedy this situation, while at the same time improving the religious studies programs.

2. *Catholic colleges and universities form men and women who will enter leadership positions in American society*—in politics, the professions, the media, and also in the Church. Professional or

even humanistic formation is not enough. What is needed is a formation based upon Catholic principles and integrated with the commitment to the Catholic faith and to the moral values derived therefrom, enabling these young men and women to have a positive influence on the various professions and on American society as a whole—and therefore on world society, since American influence in the world today is so great.

3. *Significant numbers of people today wonder whether the Catholic colleges and universities are as "Catholic" as they once were*; this is in part related to the questions of autonomy and academic freedom, which are so much discussed today. Being "Catholic" is not just a question of fidelity to Catholic doctrine; it involves the spirit of the institution, pastoral ministry, and the behavior of the students.

Each of these concerns (and again I am only indicating a few of the more serious ones) points to the need for a closer relationship between Catholic colleges and universities and the bishops—the individual institution with the bishop of the diocese in which it is located and the collection of institutions with the episcopal conference. There is much evidence to suggest that the relationship is better today than it was several years ago. But working on this relationship must still be a priority. A bishop needs to see the educational institution, including its leadership, its teachers, and its students, as one of the important elements in his diocese, offering a tremendous potential to affect the life of the diocese. ("The bishops of the Church, as *doctores et magistri fidei*, should be seen not as external agents but as participants in the life of the Catholic university in its privileged role as protagonist in the encounter between faith and science and between revealed truth and culture," Pope John Paul II, *Address to Leaders in Catholic Higher Education*, New Orleans, Sept. 12, 1987.) The directors of the institutions and, indeed, every individual within them need to see more clearly what it means to be a Catholic college or university, an institution closely related to the Church and its pastors; they need to become more clearly convinced of their own responsibility to serve the mission of the Church.

As you know, the new *Code of Canon Law* has a section on Catholic universities; in order to assist in the implementation of the Code and assist both the institutions and the bishops to address the challenges of today, the Congregation has been at work for several years preparing materials for the Holy Father from which he can publish a pontifical document on Catholic higher education. That work is nearing its completion. You have all received the latest revision of a draft document and, as you know, an international meeting will be held in April to discuss this draft. The United States, both educational institutions and bishops, will be well represented at this meeting. The discussions now going on in your country can help us in revising this draft and therefore will be of assistance to the Holy Father. But these discussions can also help the institutions to clarify their Catholic identity, can help the bishops to understand the concerns more clearly and—perhaps most important—can clarify the need for a close relationship between institutions and pastors.

Moreover, the draft asks bishops or episcopal conferences to supplement this pontifical document with documents of their own, which will apply the general norms to their own more concrete circumstances and which will further clarify both identity and relationship within the more local cultural circumstances. You have already published a significant document on pastoral life in the American colleges and universities; your work on a more comprehensive document that integrates this pastoral dimension into the entire life of the college or university can help to meet the concerns that I have noted.

Finally, I would only mention in passing the need to be concerned about the many Catholic youth who do not attend Catholic schools or who do not go on to Catholic colleges and universities. The numbers of such young people are increasing, as you know. I will not develop this concern, except to say that the responsibility of the bishop for the formation of young people must also somehow reach these young people outside of our Catholic institutions, and that new approaches for reaching all Catholic youth must be explored.

Archbishop Eugene Marino

In the recent post-synod apostolic exhortation *Christifideles Laici*, our Holy Father, Pope John Paul II, sets the focus for reflection today when he writes:

> First of all the Church is a teacher, in which the Pope takes the "primary" role in the formation of the lay faithful. As successor of Saint Peter, he has the ministry of "confirming his brothers in the faith," instructing all believers in the essential content of vocation and mission in light of the Christian faith and membership in the Church. Therefore, not simply the words coming directly from him, but also those transmitted by the various departments of the Holy See call for a loving and receptive hearing by the lay faithful (no. 61).

In this spirit, the bishops of the United States on numerous occasions have affirmed their ongoing support for all forms of Catholic education; in the tradition of the various Confraternities of Christian Doctrine, today's Church utilizes institutional opportunities at all levels to exercise her teaching mission.

In Los Angeles in 1987, His Holiness reminded us of the insight from *Catechesi Tradendae* that

> We [the bishops] serve our laity best when we make every effort to provide for them, and in collaboration with them, a comprehensive and solid program of catechesis with the aim of "maturing the initial faith and of educating the true disciple of Christ by means of a deeper and more systematic knowledge of the person and the message of our Lord Jesus Christ" (*Address to Bishops: Papal Response to Presentation by Archbishop Rembert G. Weakland, OSB*).

The bishops of the United States have, therefore, over the years issued pastoral letters on lifelong Catholic education in *To Teach as Jesus Did*; on Catholic colleges and universities in *Catholic Higher Education and the Pastoral Mission of the Church*, and on campus ministry in *Empowered by the Spirit: Campus Ministry Faces the Future*. The bishops also conducted a massive consultation which led to the publication of *Sharing the Light of Faith*, the national catechetical directory called for in the *General Catechetical Directory*. After five years of implementation, the bishops created a special committee to study the possibility of revising the directory and are presently awaiting the publication of the *Universal Catechism* before undertaking another similar study.

In the realm of the actual, American Catholic schools in 1989 are committed to teaching the Catholic faith and its values along with the secular sciences in the atmosphere of a caring community. They are committed to and largely characterized by excellent academic programs, which strive to meet the individual needs of the young in a changing society. Catholic education in the United States offers a unique alternative to pluralistic public education. Its philosophy is threefold: to teach the message of the Gospel; to build an earthly community based on Christ's command to love the Father and one another; and to serve human society through prayer, public liturgy, and social action.

Numerous studies done by independent researchers as well as by the Church attest to the fact that the Catholic school has been successful in both its religious and academic educational efforts. What is even more noteworthy is the committed presence of the Catholic schools in the inner city, where quite often they serve the very poor and minorities, many of whom are not Catholic children.

The primary and secondary Catholic school in the United States continues to be a sign of the commitment and generosity of the Catholic community to Christian education inasmuch as these schools are supported by the contributions of the faithful without any aid from the government. The bishops, together with the faithful, have worked and continue to work to correct what appears to be a basic injustice to parents who wish to choose a Catholic school for their children. Despite the hardships identified with an ongoing commitment to these schools, we are confident that the efforts of so many who are united for the sake of their children are worth the sacrifice.

Unlike their counterparts in elementary education and most of those in secondary education, Catholic colleges are supported almost totally by tuition. They survive or fail not because a diocese or a religious community will maintain a commitment to them, but rather on the pragmatic basis that they provide or fail to provide the college educational services that American students demand and are willing to pay for.

In providing Catholic services to their students, these institutions must compete with all other types of higher education—tax supported or endowment secured. It is a tribute to these colleges that they have survived and continue to thrive. The Church, and especially the bishops, generally encourage these higher education facilities and wherever possible support them.

The Christian education of youth is further enhanced by the efforts of dioceses to provide total youth ministry for teenagers, campus ministry programs for Catholic students on secular campuses, and programs for single young adults in the workplace.

In the exercise of our formative duties in educating the young, we try to be appreciative of every means that may be of service, but we must especially rely on those which are essentially the Church's own. Chief among these is catechetical instruction within the parish community, which illumines and strengthens the faith, develops a life in harmony with the spirit of Christ, stimulates a conscious and fervent participation in the liturgical mystery, and encourages young men and women to take an active part in the apostolate.

The bishops are conscious of their responsibility directly and through their presbyters and catechists to present the doctrine of faith, to clarify it, to expound it, and finally to exhort youth to put it into practice. Thus the depth and the riches of the mysteries of salvation will unfold and be seen in their critical significance for the life of the individual Catholic and for the community at large.

Pastors of souls are conscious of their grave obligation to do all in their power to ensure that Catholic education is enjoyed by all the faithful and especially by the young, who are the hope of the Church. For all of these reasons, in the words of our Holy Father in his most recent exhortation: "The Church does not tire of proclaiming Jesus Christ, of proclaiming his Gospel as the unique and satisfying response to the most deep-seated aspirations of young people" (*Christifideles Laici*, 46).

In their pastoral message on Catholic education *To Teach as Jesus Did*, the bishops of the United States renewed emphasis on the parents' role as the primary catechists of their children. The future can be discerned in the increased involvement of parents in this process and in the growth of parish-based efforts to assist parents in this responsibility. As it is the parents who have given life to their children, with them rests the gravest obligation of educating their offspring. There is no adequate substitute for the emotional, spiritual, and moral foundation acquired in the atmosphere of a loving family. We generously support the needs of all parents in their attempts to provide guidance to their children in the face of the world's uncertainties and negative forces. We must also assist parents by helping to keep their basic role clearly defined. Religious education of adults is vitally connected to the religious education of the young.

We affirm our deep gratitude to those priests, religious, and lay women and men who in a spirit of evangelical dedication have devoted themselves to the all-important and splendid work of Catholic education. We encourage them to persevere generously in what they have undertaken, and we pray that they may excel in inspiring their students with the spirit of Christ. Thus they will not only promote the internal renewal of the Church, but will also maintain and augment its beneficial presence in the world today.

To oversee, to inspire, and to animate all these facets of the Church's teaching mission is the serious duty of the bishops. As we were reminded in Los Angeles, we must seek "to release into the life stream of ecclesial life all the richness of the Church's self-understanding, which was given by the Holy Spirit to the community of faith in the celebration of the Second Vatican Council" (*Address to Bishops: Papal Response to Presentation by Joseph Cardinal Bernardin*). We must endeavor to see that this charge is carried out faithfully. We must ensure that all teachers who share this responsibility with us teach faithfully, authentically, and accurately in the spirit of Jesus Christ as it is understood by the Church through her formative office, the magisterium. The Holy Father has written in *Redemptor Hominis*:

> With deep emotion we hear Christ himself saying: "The word which you hear is not mine, but the Father's who sent me.". . . Even he, "the only Son of God," . . . when transmitting that truth as a prophet and teacher, feels the need to stress that he is acting in full fidelity to its divine source. The same fidelity must be a constitutive quality of the Church's faith, both when she is teaching it and when she is professing it. . . . Therefore it is required, when the Church professes and teaches the faith, that she should adhere strictly to divine truth and should translate it into living attitudes of "obedience in harmony with reason" (no. 19).

Seminaries and Vocations

William Cardinal Baum

The future of priestly formation in the United States will depend for its health on the reinforcement of certain features of the present system and the repair of some specific deficiencies. In the light of the apostolic visitation of 221 centers of priestly formation, the quinquennial reports of the individual dioceses, and the remarks made by bishops during their *Ad Limina* visits, the following points emerge.

1. *One of the features of the apostolic visitation which was most appreciated by the seminaries was the presence on the visitation teams of a good number of bishops.* Your episcopal presence and interest were particularly supportive, encouraging, and, indeed, directive. This reinforces an essential truth, namely that good pastoral relationships between bishops and their seminaries are not only enriching in themselves, but are a precondition and a sure foundation for the bishops' theological leadership of priestly formation. We would like to encourage further regular visits by bishops to the seminaries they use. It is particularly important that a seminary's ordinary visit it; but also the other bishops who sponsor students there should establish an understanding with the ordinary and the seminary authorities so as to be able to visit their students. Contact between diocese and seminarian is usually maintained by the vocations director, but this cannot substitute entirely for the presence of the bishop.

Apostolic visitations of priestly formation have taken place in other countries such as Italy, the Philippines, Argentina, Peru, and Brazil. At the moment we are taking the pulse of the 34 colleges here in Rome for which we are responsible. The Holy Father's review of priestly formation will continue in other countries in the near future. We have learned much from the American visitation, not only about strengths and weaknesses, but also about visitation methods and about the sociocultural context in which priestly formation takes place; and for this we express our very great thanks and appreciation.

2. *There is need for positive thinking about vocations, and there is need for a constructive approach to recruitment.* Repeated references to "the vocations crisis" can lead to a prophecy of doom which is self-fulfilling. It is true that we have seen a decline in the number of vocations to the priesthood. A similar decline occurred in other countries. A significant number of those other countries have already overcome the crisis. Numbers are rising again dramatically in Latin America, Africa, Asia, the Philippines, and Poland. They are rising healthily in Holland and West Germany, for instance, as well as elsewhere. We can expect a similar recovery in the United States; but such a recovery is not served by those who interpret the present statistics as a depressing tale of woe, but rather by those who believe in the enterprise of priesthood, and who are confident in the power of God's grace to guide and strengthen youths and young men who are waiting on his call.

A positive approach to vocations must shrug off the pressures to mute the priesthood that come from people who want women priests, married priests, part-time priests, or simply optional celibacy. We must also be careful in interpreting the decline in vocations to the priesthood as "providentially" enabling other ministries to develop in the Church. Other ministries develop most legitimately and fruitfully in those parishes where the ministry of the priest is most effectively and happily carried out. Look around your own archdioceses: Is it not true that your good, happy priests have the most vibrant, apostolic parishes, with their people most constructively involved?

3. *Vatican Council II affirmed the necessity of seminaries in order to provide a specialized formation for the priesthood.* The United States has maintained a network of seminaries at both college and theologate levels. The system is looser and more fragmented at the college level than at the theologate, yet the whole Church in the United States must be grateful to those who at great cost have maintained the seminaries, which are more necessary than ever in view of the state of American culture. When the number of vocations begins to rise again, the seminaries will come under pressure to expand, both with regard to the needs of the Church within the United States and for the missions abroad. We must maintain our commitment both to the Church at home and in those countries which need our help.

112

4. *The most important issue to have been raised by the visitation is the very idea of the priesthood.* Priestly formation in the United States, as elsewhere, must be inspired and informed by the theology of the priesthood as given to us in revelation, maintained in tradition, and protected and proposed by the magisterium; I refer especially to the documents of Vatican II and the letter of Paul VI *On Priestly Celibacy.* I also include the American *Program of Priestly Formation.* These documents are to a seminary what the Constitution and the Bill of Rights are to a law school. To have them present on the library shelf is not enough. They must inform—and be articulated in—the living tradition of the institution.

5. *If we are to have priests who will be adequate to the challenges that confront the Church in evangelizing within our contemporary culture and society as we come to the turn of the century, we must have formation programs which are thorough.* The *Decree on the Training of Priests (Optatam Totius)*, insists that candidates for the priesthood understand the biblical foundation of doctrines, their historical development, and their magisterial character and status. The curriculum of studies must facilitate this, but the proliferation of new courses has resulted in a certain theological thinness in the more essential matters which we want to correct. For example, it is not uncommon to find what used to be separate tracts on Creation and the Fall, including man and woman in the image and likeness of God, grace and justification, protology and eschatology crowded into one course of three credits.

Good professors are invaluable. We thank God for the good ones. But we not only thank God, we thank the bishops who had the perspicacity to recognize their priests' original promise and the generosity to send them for further studies, especially in those disciplines which are so central to the enterprise of priestly formation. I would draw your attention especially to the value of ecclesiastical doctorates. Conversely, I would draw your attention to a problem presented by some of the bishops during the *Ad Limina* visits: there is some concern that the system of accreditation by nonecclesiastical associations is—paradoxically—lowering our theological standards and changing our ministerial course.

6. *The provision of an adequate philosophical formation is particularly challenging, especially in view of the cultural and academic situation of our own nation.* Many of the study centers used by the many houses of formation at college level do not offer a curriculum in philosophy adequate to the needs of theology.

Sometimes theologates are constrained to accept students who have completed the minimum of 18 hours of philosophy but who still are lacking in the essential philosophical disciplines of epistemology, metaphysics, logic, ethics, etc. Those who teach philosophy and who teach it well deserve our full support. There are not enough of them though. We need to recruit more philosophers who understand philosophy's relation to theology.

7. *I want to say a word about the formation of religious candidates for the priesthood,* since the Congregation for Catholic Education has a certain competence with regard to their academic studies—their spiritual and pastoral formation being the competence of the Congregation for Religious. The quality of formation programs for religious varies greatly. Some are excellent, particularly those of the larger religious orders which have an intellectual tradition. Some of the theological unions that have been formed are rendering good service, but a number of them have yet to find a form of governance which is adequate, and some function on a rather generalized concept of ministry rather than on a specific concept of the ordained priesthood. Although there are often great talents among the professors, the curriculum of studies which some of the unions offer is philosophically very thin and theologically lacking both in content and in focus.

8. *There is much more interest these days in spirituality.* Our seminarians are thirsty for it, and they are very appreciative in particular of spiritual direction. We would like to see more attention paid to prayer, both liturgical and nonliturgical, and to popular devotions, not only for the sake of the seminarians themselves, but also for their future ministry among the people who have need of these devotions. The Mass is rightly in pride of place, but it is not the only way to worship God and the only context in which prayer takes place.

9. *Still with regard to spiritual formation, I wish to offer a comment about formation for celibacy.* Almost every seminary now treats celibacy openly and constructively, without of course invading the privacy of the students. We need to be cautious though so that it does not become problem oriented or reduced to considerations of psychosexuality and affectivity. We need to give more attention to the theological foundation of celibacy, based on the example of the Lord himself, and on the consequent spirituality. A seminarian should come to understand his call to celibacy as an invitation to give his life as an oblation to the Father and at the

service of the people of God. As St. Augustine said, admittedly in another context, "Show me a lover. He'll know what I mean." Fidelity to the promise of celibacy in our own time has a particular prophetic value, especially among those who doubt the possibility of chastity in life and fidelity in marriage. We want our seminarians to know the social significance of celibacy in Christ.

In short, this is the way we see the future: closer involvement by the bishops in their leadership of priestly formation; the maintenance of the seminary system as affirmed by and in the light of Vatican II; the promotion of a sound philosophical formation, of a theological formation which is biblical, historical, and magisterial, and of a complete priestly formation, which in its spiritual, liturgical, academic, and pastoral dimensions is informed by a thorough and well-articulated theology of the priesthood.

Archbishop Daniel Pilarczyk

In 1968, I was appointed rector of our minor seminary in Cincinnati. The seminary's program at that time was almost exactly the same as it had been when I entered there as a student 20 years previously. It soon became clear to me that the program of 1948, good as it had been, was no longer suitable for 1968. Strict confinement and lock-step training were fast becoming unintelligible to young men who had enjoyed a degree of freedom at home that was unheard of when I was a boy, and who had been taught the values of personal choice and self-determination by the culture in which they had grown up. Something had to be done to make the seminary program appropriate for this new situation.

Seminaries, both minor and major, around the country were facing the same problems. It was a difficult period because there were no time-tested patterns of successful seminary programs. The National Conference of Catholic Bishops' *Program of Priestly Formation* was not published until some years later and even then did not solve every problem or answer every question. Those of us who were responsible for seminary formation in those days had to do quite a bit of prayerful guesswork and prudent risk taking. At the same time, demonstrations and protests were taking place in seminaries across the country on the part of those who believed that the seminary was not doing enough to bring the attitudes and decisions of the Second Vatican Council into the training program for future priests. It was a difficult time in our country for seminary personnel and for the Church in general.

The results of those efforts and that turmoil are what we see now in the seminaries of the United States. I believe that these results indicate that the efforts and the turmoil were worthwhile, though not without a problematic of their own.

On the positive side, those who are ordained priests today have a much wider pastoral experience than was the case before. We have learned over the years that pastoral training is much more than simply sending students out of the seminary to "do something." The pastoral preparation of seminarians has become a highly specialized and carefully monitored part of the seminary program, including not just sporadic activity, but carefully planned experiences joined with clearly focused theological reflection. Unlike the past, today's candidates for priesthood have a much clearer idea of what is expected of them in priestly ministry and are much more skilled in providing it.

Preaching receives much more attention in the seminary program now than it did before, not just the techniques of delivery but also the theological and ascetical content of the ministry of the word.

In response to the emphasis of Vatican II on liturgy, the newly ordained of today have a far deeper insight and interest in the corporate worship of the Church than was the case before the Council.

The presentation of theological studies is different too. Instead of a series of lectures which changed little, if at all, from one year to another, the students are now made to engage in reading and reflection on their own so as to be able to come to their classes with a greater capacity for interest and assimilation.

Finally, still on the positive side, it is my impression that personal spirituality and a lively prayer life are a deeper part of the lives of seminarians today. If nothing else, younger priests seem able to speak about prayer and contact with the Lord in ways that were not at all common in the past.

This is not to say, of course, that everything in our American seminaries is beyond improvement. There are problems too. We bishops are concerned sometimes about the quality of the academic theological program at a time when so much more has been added to the seminary program and so little taken out. We wonder what the long-term effect of our culture's individualism and privatism will be on the ministries of those called to a lifetime of service to the people of God, and how that individualism and privatism can be dealt with appropriately in our formation programs. We want to be sure that a clear and orthodox idea of priesthood and priestly ministry is inculcated in those who will be our key collaborators in the years ahead.

Most of these points, both positive and negative, have already been highlighted in the pontifical visitation of our seminaries, which was concluded last year. When that visitation was first announced, it was greeted with a certain degree of apprehension. Thanks to the careful and professional way in which the visitation was carried out by Bishop Marshall and his collaborators, thanks to the generous cooperation of the seminaries themselves, and thanks to the thoughtful responses to the study by the authorities of the Holy See, we are now reassured that the strengths of our seminaries have been recognized and that the weaknesses which have been highlighted are those for which we share concern.

Now let's look for a moment at vocations to the priesthood. The one glaring fact in this context is the decline of numbers, at least relatively speaking. As I pointed out in my address to the Holy Father in Los Angeles, the ratio of priests to Catholics has grown from 771 to 920 between 1962 and 1987. The number of seminarians presently in our seminaries seems to indicate that this trend will not be reversed soon. What is the cause of this decline? What does it mean? I believe it would be presumptuous of me even to attempt to answer those questions, and I will content myself with offering still other questions to indicate where the problems may lie. How attractive is a lifetime of service in a culture which stresses self-satisfaction and in which lifetime commitment seems more and more difficult, even in marriage? What is the significance of the fact that in the past the priest was the sole authority and sole minister in the parish, whereas now decision making is shared with the parishioners, and parochial ministry is shared with lay ministers and women religious? What is the effect of rising expectations from priestly ministry on the part of the Catholic faithful? What is the real influence on vocations of the controversies about priestly celibacy and the ordination of women to priesthood? What has the general turmoil in the Church between so-called conservatives and liberals contributed to the decline in vocations? Over the last several decades, American Catholics have become one of the most highly educated and economically successful segments of our society. Does this have anything to do with fewer Catholic young men presenting themselves for priesthood? What is the effect on vocations of smaller families? Does the decline in numbers of active priests per Catholic itself have an influence on vocations? For that matter, how many priests do we really need? Is a large number of vocations to priesthood an unequivocal sign of the health of the Church? Is the decline in numbers of priests an indication of decay or a call to modify the way in which we minister to our people?

I hope that this partial list of possible questions will indicate that, in my opinion at least, there is no simple answer. It is a matter with which we will have to continue to wrestle, not without concern, but not without confidence in the Lord's love and care for his Church.

Introduction to the Holy Mass with the Bishops of the United States

His Holiness John Paul II

Dear Brothers,

It is most fitting that these days of prayer and consultation should culminate in this concelebration of the Eucharist, for it is here at the altar that the Church is revealed in her most intimate nature as a hierarchical communion of faith, hope, and love.

We celebrate this Eucharist at the tomb of St. Peter, who, together with the other apostles, was chosen by the Lord to be the foundation of his Church. The calling of these apostles is deeply related, both historically and in the order of grace, to their experience of Christ and to their profession of faith in him. As we venerate the memory of Peter, we ask his intercession that we may find the inspiration and strength we need in order to imitate the apostles in bearing courageous witness to Christ.

The Lord's words to Peter: "Do you love me? . . . Feed my lambs. . . . Tend my sheep" (Jn 21:15-17) are addressed to each of his successors, the Bishops of Rome. But they also apply to all the bishops, the successors of the apostles, who are entrusted with the care of a flock that is the Lord's and not their own. Like Peter, what is asked of us is a love that puts its full trust in God and that perseveres to the end even in the face of misunderstanding and rejection. It is the love that "bears all things, believes all things, hopes all things, endures all things" (1 Cor 13:7).

Today's liturgy reminds us once again that Christ appeared as a sign of contradiction in the midst of those whom he came to save. In the darkness and confusion created by sin, he was destined to give his life as a ransom for many (cf. Mt 20:28). Invoking the intercession of our Mother, Mary, who lived this redemptive mystery to the full, and of Sts. Peter and Paul, we pray that God will continue to pour out his blessings on the whole Church in the United

States. May he also bestow upon each of you, dear brothers, a full measure of his gifts as you seek to fulfill your mission as teachers of the faith and evangelizers in your beloved country, which is blessed with the protection of Mary Immaculate, the Mother of the Church.

Ecumenism and Evangelization

Johannes Cardinal Willebrands

There is an intimate and organic link between ecumenism and evangelization. The concern for the preaching of the Gospel to the whole creation and the concern for the unity of all Christians are both biblical concerns.

The organic link between ecumenism and evangelization is perhaps most dramatically expressed in the priestly prayer of Jesus in John 17, the text that is seen as one of the classical biblical texts that motivates us in fostering Christian unity and in evangelization as well. Jesus prayed:

> I do not pray for these only, but also for those who believe in me through their word, that they may all be one; even as thou Father art in me, and I in thee, that they may also be in us, so that the world may believe that thou hast sent me (Jn 17:20-21).

I mention two theological reflections suggested by this text. The first concerns the relationship of unity to evangelization. The only condition or consideration that Jesus emphasizes here in regard to the world, that is, the whole creation, believing that God has sent him (evangelization) is the *unity* of his disciples ("they may be one . . . the world may believe"). The intimate link between unity and evangelization in this Johannine spirit was indicated as well by the Second Vatican Council. It stated that discord among Christians "openly contradicts the will of Christ, provides a stumbling block to the world, and inflicts damage on the most holy cause of proclaiming the good news to every creature" (*Unitatis Redintegratio*, 1).

Second, in this priestly prayer there is an allusion to the deep meaning of unity. It is unity in the Father and the Son through the Holy Spirit. Jesus prays "that they may all be one; even as thou Father art in me, and I in thee, that they may also be in us. . . ." The unity between Father and Son is made in the Holy Spirit. Jesus makes his unity with the Father the source and model of those who believe in him: the unity in him and the unity among themselves.

These are not two unities; it is one. The unity of the Church is unity in the image of the Holy Trinity. The Second Vatican Council illustrated this in speaking of the sacred mystery of the unity of the Church. "The highest exemplar and source of this mystery," it said, "is the unity, in the Trinity of persons, of one God, the Father and the Son in the Holy Spirit" (*Unitatis Redintegratio*, 2). The unity of the Church belongs therefore to the mystery of the Church.

It follows from this that division among Christians is not a superficial thing. Rather it touches something at the very heart of the mystery of the Church. Surely the unity of the One, Holy, Catholic and Apostolic Church is never lost; it will always be maintained by the divine source from which it comes (*subsistit in Ecclesia catholica, a successore Petri et episcopis in eius communione gubernata,* cf. *Lumen Gentium*, 8; *Unitatis Redintegratio*, 4). Nevertheless, division among those who believe in Christ, and for whose unity Christ prayed, "inflicts damage on the most holy cause of proclaiming the good news to every creature" (*Unitatis Redintegratio*, 1). It is for this reason that the ecumenical movement is one of the ways of obedience to Christ. And the quest for the unity of Christians is closely related to the mission of the Church to preach the Gospel, to evangelize a secularized world.

The last verses of the Gospel of Matthew show the great commission given by Jesus to his followers to make disciples of all nations, baptizing them in the name of the Father, and of the Son, and of the Holy Spirit (cf. Mt 28:19-20).

The New Testament images illustrating the deep and frequent biblical concern for the unity of the followers of Christ are too numerous to list here. We can mention, for example, the Johannine image of Jesus as the Good Shepherd who seeks to bring other sheep not of the fold, "so there shall be one flock and one shepherd" (cf. Jn 10:11-16): "Jesus should die for the nation and not for the nation only but to gather into one the children of God who are scattered abroad" (Jn 11:52). Let me just refer also to the letters of St. Paul, especially the letters of the captivity. Ephesians is really the epistle of Christian unity: "There is one body and one Spirit, just as you were called to the one hope that belongs to your call, one Lord, one faith, one baptism, one God and Father of us all . . ." (Eph 4:4-6).

But besides these biblical and theological reflections, we should keep in mind also the concrete situation of ecumenism in the United States. The ecumenical movement is widespread in the

United States. It offers a great panorama of all the different approaches to ecumenism. Allow me to give some impressions and judgments on the ecumenical movement in the United States (I have some experience of the situation through international and national contacts, though it is not comparable to yours).

Many church leaders and many theologians, Catholic and non-Catholic, are seriously engaged in the search for unity. How far does this engagement reach the people in the pew and the people in the street? There are churches on nearly every street, but at the same time there is a widespread secularism. Secularism in a pragmatic society. A question arises when ecumenical documents are published and come to the people. In that case, the doctrinal office of the bishop or even of the Bishop of Rome has to watch over the faith of the people. Pragmatic and secularized society could have a negative influence. Dialogue has a teaching feature and effect, although it is different from instruction (for instance given to converts). We have the problem of language. Not only because in the 20th century we cannot speak the language of the 16th, but also because the language of Catholic theology is different from the one of Orthodox or Protestant theology. The Second Vatican Council says "the Catholic belief needs to be explained . . . in ways and in terminology which our separated brethren too can really understand" (*Unitatis Redintegratio*, 11). Precisely, therefore, dialogue is necessary. Even for ourselves we gain new insights in the encounter with other Christians. But here, not less than in other fields (renewal of liturgy), dynamics of change bring their influence to bear upon the mind and understanding of people.

The participation of the people is not limited to prayer, which is nevertheless the most important part of all ecumenical activity. Jesus prayed for unity in what we call the high-priestly prayer. People take part in much practical collaboration. They are often the main agents.

Two points at issue, always returning, are intercommunion and mixed marriages. Slowly Protestants begin to understand that the refusal of intercommunion is a demand of faith, not of human hospitality. The causal link between the one body and the one bread is understood very differently by Protestants and by Catholics.

Concerning mixed marriages, we cannot take away the difficulty and pain because their unity is not lived in full communion of faith. If the couple's acceptance of this situation in mutual love becomes a spiritual emulation, it becomes also an ecumenical occasion. Pastoral care in common understanding between the Catholic and the Protestant pastor is necessary.

Above all, we have to love our brothers and sisters in the other Christian communities. They belong to your flock in the sense of Jesus' word: "I have other sheep, they are not of this fold; I must bring them also, and they will heed my voice" (Jn 10:16). Yes, they will heed, if we speak the truth in love.

In all this, guidance and inspiration from the bishops as fathers and teachers of the faith are necessary in order that ecumenism may not degenerate in false irenicism and eventually in indifferentism. A secularized world fosters such deviation and the *princeps demoniorum* is by nature opposed to unity. But we have reason to thank God for the movement toward true unity which has created a new situation.

The duty of reevangelization is an essential one. But for the theological reasons mentioned above, as well as for the concrete situation in the United States, where an ecumenical spirit has taken root, the Church cannot neglect the work of ecumenism while it deepens its efforts at evangelization. The work for unity requires the same spiritual effort, the same patient perseverance, conviction, and hope as the work to bring all the people of the earth to the Christian faith. In a certain sense, ecumenical activity is a condition for evangelization since Christ prayed "that they all may be one, so that the world may believe."

Bishop William Keeler

Christian-Jewish Relations

Most Holy Father, at Miami you recalled God's covenant with Abraham, Isaac, and Jacob as "a very substantial starting point for our dialogue and our common witness in the world" with our Jewish brothers and sisters. As you reminded us then in the United States, with the largest Jewish population of any nation, there are remarkably durable and deepening relations with the Jewish community, both nationally and in the dioceses.

This friendship is not without challenges and divergences of perspective, stemming in the main from the tragedies of the past and, most poignantly, the *Shoah* [the Holocaust]. Jews on all levels state their concerns quite candidly with us.

We continue to hear from them regarding Catholic teaching and preaching, the Holy See and the state of Israel, and topics of mutual interest such as moral values and public education, the family, peace, and the economy, often in positive appreciation of our own efforts in these areas.

All of these topics and more have been taken up in our various relations with Jewish agencies, most formally in our twice-yearly meetings of bishops from around the country with representatives of the Synagogue Council of America, the umbrella group for religious Jewry in the United States.

Reciprocally, we have been able in our consultations with Jewish organizations to raise our own particular concerns, for example, regarding human life issues and the importance of Catholic school education. In meetings last fall and this winter, we highlighted our growing dismay over misperceptions in the media with regard to positions of the Holy See. We bishops have seen the impact of this misinformation on Jewish perceptions of Catholics.

In response, and in consultation with Cardinal Willebrands, we went directly to Jewish leaders with our concerns, seeking their assistance in clarifying the record for the Jewish community. The response has been heartening. The American Jewish Committee, the Synagogue Council of America, and the Anti-Defamation League of B'nai B'rith are all circulating very helpful memorandums of clarification to their own constituencies.

The recent document of the Pontifical Justice and Peace Commission on racism has been positively received and will be of great help to our efforts, as have the 1974 and 1985 statements of the Vatican's Commission for Religious Relations with the Jews.

To assist dioceses in implementing the latter on the local level, committees of our conference have within the past year published two major documents: *Criteria for the Evaluation of Dramatizations of the Passion*, (Bishops' Committee for Ecumenical and Interreligious Affairs, approved March 22, 1988); and *God's Mercy Endures Forever: Guidelines on the Presentation of Jews and Judaism in Catholic Preaching* (Bishops' Committee on the Liturgy, approved September 28, 1988).

Other Interreligious Concerns

Muslims, Buddhists, Hindus, and others now figure significantly in the religious landscape of the United States, as demonstrated by the Holy Father's participation in the interreligious program *"Nostra Aetate* Alive" during his 1987 visit to Los Angeles. Through our national conference and in many dioceses, interreligious discussions and meetings are being organized with increasing frequency. Native Americans are represented as well at some of these events, which are prepared from the Catholic side in accord with the principles exemplified at the Assisi Day of Peace gathering in 1986.

Christian Ecumenical Efforts

As His Eminence Cardinal Willebrands has pointed out, the *Decree on Ecumenism* of the Second Vatican Council, drawing on basic biblical and theological imperatives, which have been carried forward in the revised *Code of Canon Law*, the exhortation of the extraordinary world Synod of Bishops in 1985, and the many statements of the Holy Father, including his address to us of Region III on October 7, 1988, placed before us as bishops of the local churches in the United States and as members of our conference a very great challenge. It is the challenge of laboring for that unity in the Christian family clearly linked to evangelization, "that the world may believe."

In many ways, the bishops have sought both to respond to the challenge and to encourage the initiatives suggested by the Council.

The ecumenical situation in the United States is both complex and diverse. Each diocesan church, even those in areas near to one another, is faced with a different ecumenical and interreligious situation. For example, in some of our largest cities, whether in the Northeast or the far West, there are large Catholic populations, some much smaller Protestant church bodies represented, and, affecting very much developments in cities and in neighborhoods, a significant presence of Jewish people.

The Protestants in one typical area might pertain to the traditions of the confessional churches of Europe, known in their American equivalents generally as "mainline churches," or to the conservative evangelical churches with roots in the frontier days of the United States and membership centered mainly in the South. Through much of the country in the smaller cities and towns, the Protestant representation is strong and active.

Established by the American bishops in 1964, the Bishops' Committee for Ecumenical and Interreligious Affairs seeks to establish and maintain relationships with other Christian churches and other religious communities at the national level, to advise and assist dioceses in developing and applying ecumenical policies, and to maintain liaison with corresponding offices of the Holy See—the Councils for Christian Unity and non-Christian Religions.

The valiant efforts of bishop committee members and staff, including Cardinals Baum and Law, the first executive directors for the office, have led to the establishment of consultations and dialogues involving other churches at the national level. These dialogues go forward, co-chaired by Catholic bishops and with the participation of scholars in the sacred sciences representing the Catholic Church on the one hand and similar delegations representing some 30 other churches or traditions on the other. Our dialogue partners report a combined membership totaling nearly 50 million. Twenty-eight bishops take part as co-chairmen or as members of dialogues or consultations sponsored on a regular basis by the BCEIA.

These dialogues generally treat theological issues of mutual interest, much like the practice in the international dialogues. Nor have moral issues been neglected: In the setting of the annual Catholic-Lutheran Bishops' Consultation, in an extended dialogue series with churches of the Reformed tradition (Roman Catholic-Presbyterian consultation group, North American Area Council of the World Alliance of Reformed Churches, 1976-1979), and now with the United Methodist Church, contemporary moral issues relating to human life concerns and bioethics have been treated extensively. In addition, and perhaps more practically, these moral issues are a constant subject of local, diocesan, and regional ecumenical meetings.

1. *The Catholic-Lutheran Dialogue*, now co-chaired by Archbishop Stafford, has held 53 meetings since 1965. Their agreed statements, including a very fundamental one on Justification by Faith, have been received as contributions by the International Commission for Catholic-Lutheran Dialogue and are widely studied. In addition, the national consultation between Catholic and Lutheran bishops has been meeting annually for the past 14 years and is now listing ways, short of full communion, whereby we may demonstrate a growing spirit of mutual trust and active cooperation.

2. *The Orthodox-Catholic Theological Consultation*. Begun in 1966, this has met 37 times and issued 16 agreed statements. In recent years, it has been complemented by the consultation between Catholic and Orthodox bishops co-chaired by Archbishop Rembert Weakland, OSB. This past year, the bishops' consultation, at its seventh meeting, issued its own first agreed statement, on the priesthood.

Notably warmer relationships have developed in recent years with the Orthodox throughout our country. During the Marian Year, in many places, local Orthodox bishops cooperated with our bishops in special studies and devotions in honor of Mary, the Mother of God.

3. *Anglican-Roman Catholic Commission*. This dialogue began in 1966 and is now co-chaired by Archbishop John Whealon. In addition to agreed statements, the commission has reflected on the work of the Anglican-Roman Catholic International Commission from an American perspective. The decision of the Lambeth Conference regarding the ordination of women to the episcopate was the occasion of a statement by Archbishop Stafford, chairman of the BCEIA, who indicated the ecumenical difficulties which would be occasioned by such a step.

4. *Other dialogues* include those with the Polish National Catholic Church and the Oriental Orthodox Churches, both uniquely developed in the United States.

The BCEIA has also facilitated:

- Catholic participation in an annual meeting of Christian church leaders, including many leaders of churches with which we do not have regular exchanges;
- relationships with the National Council of Churches;
- Catholic participation in national level ad hoc ecumenical consultations; and
- responses from the United States to official inquiries for reactions to the results of the international dialogues.

Recent years have seen the strengthening of national ecumenical networks and a movement toward organizational unity involving large Protestant churches such as, for example, the formation of the new Evangelical Lutheran Church in America out of three smaller groups.

In the last decade an ecumenical dimension has appeared in the pro-life movement in the United States, with the growth of nonsectarian but largely Christian pro-life organizations. Especially strong is an ecumenical anti-pornography effort involving at the national level the leadership of almost all Christian churches.

Regional, State and Diocesan, and Local Activities

These are often patterned on the national models. Situations vary greatly from place to place depending on such factors as the relative size of the Catholic Church, the ecclesiology and structure of other Christian churches, and local attitudes of leaders and lay members.

At the local level, especially, encouraged by the example and the exhortation of the Holy Father and the bishops, the spiritual ecumenism of which Cardinal Willebrands spoke is broadly practiced. Both in ecumenical services and in private and public Catholic prayer (e.g., in the general intercessions of the Eucharist) the intention of unity is lifted up to the Lord. Members of the Focolare Movement and many others seek to foster spiritual ecumenism. In addition, there are numerous local ecumenical projects expressing a common concern for works of charity and justice, including efforts on behalf of the hungry and the homeless.

As I mentioned when we began to prepare for the Holy Father's visit two years ago, bishops in the United States must consider these realities:

1. The content and language of authoritative church teaching regarding ecumenism and also specific ecumenical efforts are not generally known or appreciated at the parish level. However, the Catholic press and the implementation of the *Ecumenical Directory* and local guidelines have been helpful in making many aware of the general thrust of the ecumenical movement. Seminary programs on ecumenism, some still at the beginning stages, received positive encouragement from the visitation of our bishops carried out at the request of the Holy Father. Also, surveys indicate that Catholic laity view ecumenism as a positive fruit of the Second Vatican Council, even though many may not be involved in specific ecumenical activities.

2. To the extent that ecumenism is "good news," positive and sometimes complex ecumenical developments are not adequately reported in the general news media. In the light of this problem, 3 and 4 below can be better understood.

3. Although mixed marriages pose a special problematic, some significant steps have been taken at promoting understanding between church bodies regarding points at issue.

4. At the community level, in general, people of all churches frequently raise questions about the possibility of eucharistic sharing. The *Guidelines for Receiving Communion* approved in 1986 by our Administrative Committee represent an effort to clarify the matter for Catholics who participate regularly at Mass.

5. Further complications stem from the presence of certain independent conservative evangelical churches, which are generally hostile to the Catholic Church as well as to mainline Protestant churches and to anything "ecumenical." There are also widely broadcast TV and radio programs supporting this same point of view. Especially among Hispanic Catholics, such groups, together with Pentecostal churches and some others, have made serious inroads. The BCEIA is working with the National Conference of Catholic Bishops to address these issues.

Reflections on the Papal Visit

The bishops of the United States are deeply appreciative of the time which the Holy Father took during his 1987 visit to address the ecumenical dimension of our pastoral life.

The Holy Father's private meeting at Columbia, S.C., with 26 representatives of Anglican, Orthodox, and Protestant churches was very positively commented on by those who participated. The Holy Father's spontaneous reference to this meeting, which took place on the second floor of a building, as an "Upper Room experience" touched by the presence of the Holy Spirit reflected accurately the sentiments of those present. Many bishops of our conference hope that there can be some way of following up on this Columbia meeting, perhaps with a meeting here in Rome between representatives of the congregations and councils and the Holy Father on the one hand, and representatives of this very broad group of Christian leadership on the other.

Following up on Columbia is to be a concern which probably will be expressed also on the occasion of a visit of the leadership of the National Council of Churches to Rome in April.

We know too that the public Service of the Word at which the Holy Father preached and in which most of the other church leaders took part—an unprecedented event in a state where the Catholic population is so small—was received with great faith and enthusiasm by the 60,000 participants. Eighty percent of the tickets distributed went through Protestant channels. Many times the congregation interrupted the Holy Father's message with their warm applause.

Millions around the country were able to follow this event, as others in the visit of the Holy Father, by cable television; they too found it an occasion for inspiration and ecumenical education. Incidentally, several of these Protestant leaders who participated told us afterward that they were very grateful for the moral force of the presentation of the Holy Father, including his words on marriage and the family.

At Columbia, the common statement of the 26 Christian leaders presented to the Holy Father concluded by expressing a "common desire to witness to faith in Jesus Christ" in a shared concern for moral values, a "concern for the evangelical mission of the Church," and the hope that we might "work together to make the dawn of

131

the third millennium since the advent of Christ a special time for deepening signs of unity, mission, and common witness in the world on behalf of the Gospel of Jesus Christ" (Statement read by Bishop Philip R. Cousin, September 11, 1987). All of these are expressions consonant with our theme this week. The task of pursuing unity remains a great one, linked to evangelization "that the world may believe."

The Unchurched and the Utilization of the Mass Media for Evangelization

Archbishop John Foley

It is a particular privilege for me to discuss with the spiritual leaders of my native country a theme which has long had a special significance for me: "Unchurched Persons and the Utilization of the Mass Media for Evangelization."

As you know, it is estimated that there are more than 70 million Americans who profess belief in God but who have no formal religious affiliation. It is also estimated that there are in the United States more than 15 million inactive Catholics who—for all practical purposes—may also be considered unchurched.

How can such individuals be reached, especially through the communications media?

Before I was ever given this responsibility in Rome, I was a member of the Communications Committee of the United States Catholic Conference, and I had actually proposed a program of evangelization through the communications media. One priest told me then that we were not ready to evangelize, that we were a divided Church, not ready to welcome new members. But I remain convinced, as I know you are convinced, that—if we are to be faithful to Jesus Christ—we must evangelize. I am also convinced that a concerted effort to communicate the good news of Christ provides an occasion to deepen the faith of Catholics, to heal internal divisions, and to give a renewed sense of mission within the Church.

The most recent plenary meeting of our commission, now a council, emphasized the need for national and diocesan pastoral plans for communications and for the inclusion of a communications dimension in every general pastoral plan, especially in evangelization.

Beginning with inactive Catholics, there seems to be a certain religious nostalgia between Thanksgiving and Christmas. It is a teachable moment—better, a moment when inactive Catholics are reachable.

Effective communications campaigns based on the theme "Come Home at Christmas" have been conducted in many dioceses. These include spot announcements on radio and TV and advertisements in newspapers, on billboards, and in public transportation. They also include public relations campaigns featuring stories in newspapers and on radio and TV news programs about what it means to find again faith, meaning in life, and an awareness of God's love.

Lent is another teachable moment for Catholics. It is a time when they are open to being reminded that they should share their faith.

I would suggest a radio retreat during Lent, giving Catholics a renewed appreciation for their faith and a renewed sense of urgency in sharing it. Not only could the retreat be on the radio, but it could be made available on audiocassettes for use in cars, in kitchens, and in classrooms. It might also be coordinated with the Lenten Sunday homilies in church.

Most people—whether they belong to a church or not—are aware of Holy Week and Easter. I would suggest buying time on TV and radio stations during Holy Week for a series of outstanding programs about what Catholics believe about God, about Christ, and about the Church. Let the series be promoted by newspaper advertisements and by radio and TV spot announcements. Billy Graham does it; why can't we?

Perhaps such an effort will reach a proportionately small audience in terms of the potential of the mass media, but it will probably reach more people than will be in all the parish churches in our dioceses on Holy Thursday and Good Friday. We make great efforts to offer liturgies which will touch the hundreds who come to each parish church on those days; what efforts do we make to reach the thousands and even millions of hearts which may be especially open to the message of Christ on those days so sacred to us?

A series of programs during Holy Week about what Catholics believe could be followed by a series of spot announcements on TV and radio after Easter, inviting all who are interested to "open houses" in Catholic churches on Pentecost Sunday to see the inside of a Catholic church, to see how their Catholic neighbors worship, and to hear what they believe.

Ideally, such radio or TV campaigns should support a program in which teams of Catholics visit every home and offer a warm and gracious invitation to their neighbors to visit the local Catholic church. On the occasion of such visits, printed invitations can be left also at the homes where no one answers the door, together with the prayer of St. Francis, "Lord, make me an instrument of your peace." Where home visits are impossible, telephone invitations to such parish open houses are almost always possible.

There are other methods of reaching out to the unchurched through the mass media:

- inspirational spot announcements on radio and television;

- radio phone-in programs in which well-trained and compassionate experts answer questions about the Catholic faith;

- publicizing a telephone ministry through 800 or 900 numbers in which trained respondents offer information and perhaps consolation;

- publicizing the fact that recorded spiritual messages are available on 800 or 900 numbers;

- advertising the availability of videocassettes, audiocassettes, and booklets which explain the Catholic faith, as the Knights of Columbus have done so effectively for so long;

- public relations programs which make known through the mass media what the Church is doing and what individual Catholics are doing for the poor, the sick, the handicapped, the troubled;

- regular use of the currently existing cable networks: Catholic Telecommunications Network of America, Eternal Word Television Network, and VISN—for informative programming of greater depth than is possible on broadcast stations;

- use of other teachable and reachable moments when there is a high level of curiosity about the Church—such as the installation of a new bishop, a diocesan synod, or a particular event in Rome—to explain in newspapers and on radio and TV what we believe, why we believe it, and what Jesus means to us.

Liturgical programs can sometimes offer such opportunities. We have been told by NBC, for example, that the Holy Father's

Midnight Mass at Christmas is the most popular religious program of the year in the United States. As the person responsible for the English-language commentary for that program, I personally try to remember what an opportunity that offers not only to deepen the faith of Catholics, but to touch the hearts of those who may be curious, who may be searching, and who tune in looking for consolation and perhaps for faith.

At a meeting such as this, one of the translators said to me that he had been led into the Church by the gentle commentary of the late Bishop Agnellus Andrew, who as vice president of the Pontifical Commission for Social Communications continued the work he had done for so long with the BBC in providing commentary for papal ceremonies.

We know that there are men and women who have some faith but no church and who are looking for the way home.

I am convinced that the Church in every country, but especially in the United States, should make an effort—a national effort—through the communications media to reach out to the homeless—to those without a spiritual home.

The program should be national because the need is national; there are unchurched in every state and in every diocese. A national program makes it possible to share resources and to take advantage of national publicity and momentum and of moments of special grace.

We are not alone in reaching out to the unchurched. Zealous fundamentalists and representatives of sects and cults are making great inroads among the young and the impressionable. Their personal contacts are often supplemented by TV and radio programs and by periodical literature.

We know that faith comes through hearing. Perhaps some or even most will be deaf to our message. We are not to blame if others are deaf; we are to blame if we are mute. We are mute if we do not use the communications media to proclaim Jesus, who alone is the way, the truth, and the life.

Edmund Cardinal Szoka

It is both a distinct privilege and a tremendous challenge to address the topic of the evangelization of the unchurched through the communications media.

In our pastoral ministry, each of us spends a great deal of time traveling by air. TV antennas and satellite towers now dominate the landscape where crosses on church steeples once held reign. This image is an excellent reminder that, as Christians, we live in the midst of a secular society that is at best indifferent to religion. As you have recently explained, Holy Father, our society needs reevangelization, "the formation of mature ecclesial communities in which the faith might radiate and fulfill the basic meaning of adherence to the person of Christ and His Gospel. . . ."[1]

The picture is not, however, without hope. In the eternal struggle to proclaim the Gospel, our century has been blessed with the special gift of the mass means of communication and through them the Church can find "a modern and effective version of the pulpit."[2]

Evangelization and the mass media have much in common. As means of communication, both have as their goal the creation of a true dialogue between persons.[3]

To engage the unchurched in the "dialogue of salvation,"[4] we must understand their needs and allow them to speak to us. Since communication involves both the hearer and the speaker, I will divide my presentation into three sections: (1) the unchurched themselves; (2) the Church's present efforts at reaching out to the unchurched in America; (3) some concluding principles for future discussions.

The Unchurched: Active Recipients and Participants in the Dialogue of Salvation

Although statistics vary, according to 1988 surveys,[5] approximately 78 million American adults are *unchurched*. Persons are considered *unchurched* if they are not members of a church or have not attended church services in the previous six months other than special religious holidays, weddings, or funerals. As much as 40 percent of the adult American population is probably unchurched.

It is important to note that in many cases the unchurched indicate faith in Jesus Christ, but are not interested in joining a particular church. While the number of "belongers" has declined, the number of "believers" has increased.[6]

The unchurched have religious sensibilities and in many cases they are alienated believers who are considering a return to the practice of their faith. Seventeen million of these 78 million unchurched are inactive Catholics. While there is no single reason why they have left the Church (or even why many choose to return), one of the crucial factors is always personal witness.[7]

The Church's Outreach in Communicating with the Unchurched

The Catholic Church in the United States has made tremendous commitments of finances and personnel toward understanding and appreciating the unchurched and how to communicate with them. At the present time, the Church supports: The National Catholic News Service; 156 diocesan newspapers; 5 national newspapers; and 335 religious magazines. Countless films, filmstrips, audio- and videocassettes are produced and made available through several publishing houses.[8]

In 1981, the U.S. bishops established the Catholic Telecommunications Network of America, a satellite distribution center which transmits TV and radio programs to 120 affiliates for 32 hours per week and provides facilities for disseminating electronic mail, teleconferences, and other data services. Although much of its pastoral programming is intended for internal church consumption, the capabilities of CTNA have great potential for wider outreach through redistribution on local cable systems.

Working in collaboration with CTNA, the Eternal Word Television Network (Mother Angelica) reaches 12 million cable households, with 24-hour-a-day programming.[9] Most dioceses of the country offer a weekly Mass for Shut-ins which receives a wide viewing audience.

Your 1987 pastoral visit to the United States, Holy Father, reached 20 million cable homes and represents one of the finest examples of how the resources of the media can be combined with personal witness to truly communicate the "dialogue of salvation."

Practicing and nonpracticing Catholics alike receive their basic information about the Church from the secular media. This means that attempts at outreach entail close collaboration with the secular media. Many positive steps have been taken in this regard. For instance, the presence of the various media representatives at meetings of our National Conference of Catholic Bishops has helped them to understand the complexity of the issues at hand. When properly informed, they can be a tremendous asset in communicating the Church's teaching. I am sure that the other bishops join me in thanking you, Holy Father, and the members of the Curia for the sensitivity you show to the media.

Some Concluding Principles for Evangelizatizing the Unchurched

I conclude by offering three principles for further reflection.

1. *The medium is the message.* During the Second Vatican Council, when drafts of the eventual *Decree on the Means of Social Communication* were being discussed, one of the bishops rightfully acknowledged that people of our day are influenced more by image than by abstract thought. In a very real sense, we face a paradox: to communicate faith—something which cannot be seen—we must use the senses. The good news must be proclaimed in visible, concrete ways, especially in and through the "flesh and blood" witness of believers.

2. *The proclamation of the message of faith—even to the unchurched—must always be a dialogue.*[10] Some mechanism for interchange must be built into any use of the mass media for evangelization. We must truly understand the unchurched, and, as Archbishop Foley pointed out, we must see our efforts as a response to their inner hunger and thirst. Unlike Protestant televangelists, our ultimate goal is a relationship with Jesus Christ through a commitment to the Church. Such an emphasis on community is especially necessary for evangelization among Hispanic people.[11]

3. *When it comes to evangelization, the mass media have great potential but also certain limitations.* The United States is a media-defined culture. An average American watches about four and one-half hours of television each day. Apart from sleep and work, most people spend almost 80 percent of their lives immersed in the world

of television.[12] This is particularly true for those who are senior citizens. On the other hand, there are also limitations with respect to use of the media, especially television. Some difficulties are of a practical nature: With the deregulation of the media, free service time is no longer available and public television time is extremely expensive. Cable systems, while reaching millions of homes, are still limited. An even more important limitation of television is that it does not really change people's views; it only reinforces already existing attitudes.

In view of these findings, it appears that for evangelization, the media is best used as a complement to the personal approach. Since the real value of telecommunications is more evocative than rational, it needs the personal witness of believers, particularly recent converts. The most effective way to stimulate faith among unchurched persons through the mass media is by means of 30-second TV or radio spots. In our own day no less than in the time of Jesus, parables and personal stories are still the most effective means of outreach.

In the last analysis, it is in and through our more than 19,000 parish communities of 53 million active Catholics that the Word takes flesh and the "dialogue of salvation" between churched and unchurched takes place.

Notes

1. Pope John Paul II, *Christifideles Laici,* 34.

2. Pope Paul VI, *Evangelii Nuntiandi,* 45. See also Vatican II, *Inter Mirifica,* 2-3.

3. See Pontifical Commission for Social Communications, *Communio et Progressio,* 15 and 81, and U.S. Catholic Conference Administrative Board, *In the Sight of All, Communications: A Vision All Can Share,* 9 and 12.

4. Pope Paul VI, *Ecclesiam Suam,* 81.

5. See *The Unchurched American,* a Gallup Research Study, sponsored by the Paulist National Catholic Evangelization Association, 1988, p. 1.

6. See ibid. pp. 2-3.

7. See *Attitudes of Unchurched Americans toward the Roman Catholic Church,* the Gallup Organization, Inc., 1985, pp. 55ff. See also Alvin A. Illig, CSP, "Getting a Handle on Evangelization in America," *The Living Light,* 16:1 (Spring 1979). See also Dean R. Hoge, *Converts, Dropouts, Returnees: A Study of Religious Change among Catholics,* 1981.

8. See *In the Sight of All,* p. 13.

9. See Robert P. Waznak, "The Church's Response to the Media 25 Years After *Inter Mirifica,*" *America* (January 21, 1989), p. 38.

10. See *Communio et Progressio,* 48, and *In the Sight of All,* 12. Both documents underscore the fact that media should be used in such a way as to foster an active response. See also *What We Have Seen and Heard, A Pastoral Letter on Evangelization from the Black Bishops of the United States,* p. 2.

11. See *The Unchurched American,* section on Race and Ethnicity.

12. See Robert P. Waznak, p. 40.

Brief Synthesis of the Conclusions of the Discussion by Joseph Cardinal Bernardin

To sum up a "summation" is indeed a challenge. Having listened these past few days to a variety of excellent presentations on the main issues challenging us as bishops/teachers/evangelists and the thoughtful comments offered by those ministering in particular communities and those responsible for advising the Holy Father in his overall responsibilities to the universal Church is like having listened to a symphony—at times it might have sounded like Brahms, at other times like Bartok.

However, we have been privileged to sit with our Holy Father, to share these experiences. As diocesan bishops, we are reminded of all that is left undone, all that needs to be coordinated or initiated once we have completed our quinquennial reports and leave them as but one piece in the mosaic that is the Church. We go with renewed admiration for the scope of responsibilities that are those of the Holy Father in his care for the universal flock.

What is it then that we have learned? What is it that we have tried to express? What is it that we will take with us as we return to our pastoral responsibilities?

First, we have experienced a healthy, energizing moment of mutual support—a time of reinforcement—an expression of truly pastoral love and solidarity. We have gathered in a sanctuary of trust and have felt comfortable to offer challenges, to express our concerns, to speak frankly about what binds us together, the Gospel of Jesus Christ.

We have not developed a litany of answers or solutions. We have not developed a specific program for action. Rather, in union with our Holy Father, we have opened ourselves to the Spirit, expressing at times anxieties and frustrations, at times our hope and jubilation. The root of these different emotions, of course, is simply the fact that the Gospel is one and we, though one, are many.

I will now highlight some of the principal ideas which emerged during our discussions. Obviously, this cannot be a complete summary, so extensive and rich was our exchange.

The Bishop as Teacher of the Faith

The bishop, as shepherd, is a teacher, a preacher of the Gospel, an evangelist. Some today, however, would minimize this responsibility, seeing the bishop as a spiritual administrator instead. *De facto*, others—such as professional catechists and theologians—seem to have a greater influence than he. It is essential that the bishop exercise his role as teacher with courage, fully confident with the Word he preaches. He must have the wisdom to distinguish between the essentials of the faith, which may demand definitive intervention on his part, and those matters which may legitimately be argued. When the truth is at stake, he must be willing to defend it, despite the difficulties.

To assist the bishop as teacher, a number of issues need further exploration and action:

- clarification of the role of the theologian;
- how to distinguish between the faith, which is one, and theological expressions, which may admit of a certain plurality or diversity;
- greater clarification of the levels of authority at which church teaching is presented;
- the limits of "compromise" in addressing various realities in today's society, which is sometimes needed to remain in the public debate and influence public morality;
- a better understanding of conscience formation, especially as it relates to church teaching;
- a better understanding of the educative (or pedagogical) process which will lead people more effectively from where they are to where they should be;
- a deeper understanding of the dynamics of change, so as to prepare people better for the continued implementation of Vatican II (something which was done inadequately when the implementation began nearly 25 years ago);

- the establishment of a closer connection between the scriptural cycle of the liturgy and the Church's teachings so homilies can become a more effective means of teaching.

Even as the difficulties were discussed, many spoke of the significant accomplishment of the U.S. bishops as teachers in the two centuries of our existence as a nation.

Priests as Agents of Evangelization

The bishop as evangelist to his priests must realize that they are in the front ranks of ministry and that they both need and deserve personal reaffirmation. A bishop must be close to his priests, concerned about their formation prior to ordination and after. Their spiritual formation in today's secularized culture is a priority, that they may find joy in their faith life, their ministry, their eucharistic life. They must be men of prayer, not managers.

Culture is not static, hence the priest must continue in study and personal development. Neither can we speak of a single American culture. There are multiple layers, some deeply secularized, some of a religious nature. A sense of cultures beyond his own will be for the priest the bedrock of a missionary spirit.

To be secure in his priestly identity, it is necessary that one have a sound grasp of the doctrine of priesthood, what it means to stand *in persona Christi*, a clear ecclesiology, and a firm grounding in philosophy. A sense of the mystery and the sacramental dimension of his vocation is necessary for a true understanding and appreciation of priesthood.

The priest is responsible for the education and formation of his people, in a special way that of his catechists and lay leaders. It is important that this relationship to lay leadership be clearly understood lest, on the one hand, he should fail to involve lay leaders adequately in virtue of their baptismal call to ministry or, on the other hand, contribute to the "clericalization" of the laity in a way that would blur the distinction between ordained and non-ordained service to the Church and the community. In this respect, there is a linkage between the Synod of 1987 and the upcoming Synod of 1990.

To encourage vocations to the priesthood, the bishop must work closely with his priests, for it is through their mutual example and appeal that they will encourage others to follow in their footsteps. We are supported in this by our Holy Father's apostolic exhortations to priests on Holy Thursday, and it was suggested that one of these exhortations be devoted almost exclusively to expressing encouragement, gratitude, and love for our priests.

Pastoral Responsibilities Relative to Religious Life

There was a clear affirmation of religious life as a precious gift to the Church while, at the same time, great concern was expressed about the present status of religious life in the United States. The bishop has responsibility for encouraging and defending religious life in his diocese.

The exempt status of religious congregations does not imply that religious are on the periphery of the local church. Indeed, the study of religious life which was initiated several years ago by the Holy Father was instrumental in bringing together bishops and religious in a way that was beneficial to both.

There is need for clear teaching about religious life. There are two basic orientations in religious life today: one stresses mission and ministry; the second stresses consecration and community. It is important that they be kept in balance. Religious are to be esteemed for *who* they are, apart from the apostolic works in which they are engaged—however good and needed they may be.

The bishop can be a teacher/evangelist in many ways: (1) by his own preaching, catechesis, personal presence, etc.; (2) by taking personal interest in intercongregational centers of formation and theological unions; (3) by providing clear teaching for priests on the value of religious life and meaning of eschatological witness so that they will better understand religious life and be motivated to support it.

It was also suggested that bishops consider new forms of consecrated life, especially as these relate to the diocese. Greater attention must also be given to contemplative religious.

Two particular issues elicited much concern and discussion. The first dealt with the status of the Leadership Conference of Women Religious and its relationship to the *Consortium Perfectae Caritatis*. While there were differences as to how this matter should be resolved, there was strong agreement that there must be better communication between the two and somehow a reconciliation must be brought about. Within our dioceses we must work with and involve all religious regardless of their affiliation.

The second issue was the effect of radical secular feminism on the teaching of the Church, on religious life, vocations, liturgy, etc. A number of examples of the impact of such feminism were given. There is an urgent need for a sound philosophical theological critique of this type of feminism.

Liturgy and Sacraments with Special Emphasis on the Sacrament of Reconciliation

As the Holy Father has indicated, there is an organic link between the renewal of the Church and liturgical renewal. A great grass-roots movement of catechesis in the earliest days made this renewal a reality, despite small vocal pockets of resistance. There still remains the need for ongoing catechesis and development in order that the liturgical renewal may move forward in sound fashion. It is the bishop's task to oversee this renewal and to exercise his responsibility in a timely fashion.

Certain specific liturgical issues were highlighted:

1. *First confession / first communion.* It was suggested that perhaps a special rite might be developed for children (while retaining the proper sequence in the celebration of the two sacraments) in light of the expressed concerns of parents and others. It was stated later, however, that a decision has been made not to multiply rites for children for fear that the transition from such special rites to the regular ones could be problematic.

2. *Inclusive language* can and should be incorporated into the liturgy as long as it does not impinge on scriptural or doctrinal matters. This requires careful study.

3. *Altar girls.* It was suggested that the present norm is a source of confusion to many women in the United States who are not radical feminists, but who perceive an incongruity in permitting women to serve as lectors or extraordinary ministers of the Eucharist while excluding their daughters from this lesser level of participation. It was pointed out that the norm regarding this

matter is still in effect but that, at the request of the recent synod, *Ministeria Quaedam* is being restudied.

4. *Traditionalists*. Concern was expressed as to the rationale for placating a small but vocal number of people who sidestep the local bishop's authority and, at times, seek to undermine that authority. They would appear to present a distorted image of liturgical life in the United States and absorb a disproportionate amount of time that could be better given to other more urgent matters. In regard to the Tridentine Mass, it was made clear that the hesitation to permit its more frequent use is not with the Mass *per se*, which was the center of the Church's liturgical life for so many centuries. Rather, it is the attitude of some of those who request the Mass toward the local ecclesial authority as well as toward many of the authentic developments introduced by the Second Vatican Council.

5. *General absolution*. While all were in agreement that individual auricular confession is the norm which must be observed, some suggested that the use of general absolution could be a vehicle for bringing people back to auricular individual confession. This was challenged by the experience described in at least two dioceses. A question was raised as to whether a limited, controlled experiment with Rite III in certain selected dioceses might be authorized to determine whether it would indeed revive the practice of auricular confession. It was pointed out, however, that such an experiment would not be proper because, for doctrinal reasons, the Church is not free to change the modality of the celebration of the sacrament. A further question was raised as to whether only "physical" difficulty should be taken into account as a condition for the use of Rite III—or whether moral and psychological difficulty might also be considered. It was suggested that that be studied.

Laity as Agents of Evangelization

Overall, there is a sense that considerable progress has been made in preparing the laity for church ministry (*ad intra*). However, we have been less successful in the formation of laity for their mission in the world (*ad extra*). It was suggested that a mixed commission might be established to address the manner in which the laity might be more effectively involved in the evangelization of culture, particularly in the areas of the media, art, entertainment, economics, academia, etc. In a special way, the laity are the ones who should provide the Catholic presence in the political arena.

To be agents of evangelization, the laity must be given adequate formation. They must be well instructed in the faith, especially moral teaching. They must also know *how* to collaborate with the clergy and religious.

Other groups or issues requiring special consideration include special movements and associations, women's concerns and the large number of alienated or fallen-away Catholics. In regard to the latter, it is important that we analyze the reasons for their alienation so that we will know how to reach out to them effectively.

The Family

It is evident that culture has a strong impact on family life. In the United States this involves such factors as the influence of the mass media, whose values often are in contradiction to the values of traditional family life; the development of an underclass with large numbers of single-parent families; the ongoing sexual revolution; exaggerated individualism; etc.

Special attention must be given to improved marriage preparation courses, with particular focus on the sacramentality of marriage. As bishops, we must be vigilant regarding the content of marriage preparation programs.

Although there are more marriages per 1,000 people in the United States than elsewhere, we must work against the perception of our country as a "divorce society." The number of annulments in the United States surpasses those of other nations. While concern was expressed about this, a number of bishops gave the reasons for this large number. Many cultural factors must be taken into account. The bishops of the United States are convinced that our tribunals are following the norms and procedures of the revised *Code of Canon Law* and would welcome any review on the part of the Signatura.

In regard to young people, special vigilance is needed to address the problems emanating from school-based clinics and pornography, while developing sound guidelines for education in human sexuality—a project which is under way.

Christian Education of Youth

The United States takes justifiable pride in the rich heritage of the school system that has been put in place, ranging from pre-elementary through university levels. It is the largest private school system in the world. It is a precious asset, very much related to the Church's work of evangelization, which deserves the continued support of the entire Catholic community.

As regards elementary and secondary education, strong advances have been made in attending to the Catholic identity of our schools. The *National Catechetical Directory* aided in this. But ongoing review of the syllabus for catechists, attention to the formation of teachers, involvement of parents, and the personal interaction of the bishop with the educational process are necessary. The *Universal Catechism* will be an added asset.

The financial concerns of maintaining our current elementary and secondary schools pose a major problem, at times absorbing as much as 60 percent of parish income. Long-range planning must take into consideration added revenue generation, endowments, pursuit of public aid for parents of Catholic school children, and, where necessary, consolidation. The special grace of our inner-city schools is their ability to provide quality education for minorities and the poor. But we should not lose sight of the need to provide similar educational opportunities for our Catholics who live in the suburbs, many of which do not have Catholic schools. Moreover, while the discussion focused mainly on Catholic schools, there is also an urgent need to provide quality religious education and formation for our Catholic youth who do not attend Catholic schools. They indeed are the majority.

As regards Catholic colleges and universities, many concerns are similar to those expressed above (e.g., Catholic identity, finances, etc.). Again, the close relationship between the bishop and the college/university was stressed as priority. As regards the pontifical document on Catholic higher education which is in preparation, it is important that a climate be established at the forthcoming congress which is sensitive to the very real concerns of the college/university administrators (relating to such issues as Catholic identity, academic freedom, etc.). The deliberations of the congress as well as the final document should reflect the fact that the concerns of the Holy See, the bishop, and the leadership of the colleges and the universities are mutual and not adversarial. Assurance was given that this would be done. It was pointed out, as the Holy Father had indicated earlier in New Orleans, that neither the Holy See nor the local bishop should be considered *external* to the Catholic educational institution.

Seminaries and Vocations

Again, the personal involvement of the bishop with the seminary and indeed with his seminarians is a priority of episcopal ministry. The recent pontifical visitation of the seminaries in the United States was a positive and affirming experience. Although the decline in the number of candidates remains a concern, there are positive signs as well as reasons for optimism, both in terms of the quality of present candidates and renewed vigor in vocation recruitment. In this connection, concern was expressed about overreliance on purely sociological projections, minimizing if not totally ignoring the faith context in which vocations should be encouraged.

Special attention must be paid to the issue of celibacy. The value of celibacy has been seriously eroded in our culture. There is need to develop a rationale for celibacy which will be more credible and appealing in our times for both priests and laity, given the realities which confront us.

Academically, greater stress must be placed on philosophical preparation of theological studies as well as a strengthening of the theological curriculum. This would follow logically upon the report of the pontifical visitation and could perhaps be achieved through a collaborative effort on the part of the Congregation and the episcopal conference.

Ecumenism and Evangelization

As the Church in the United States deepens its efforts at evangelization, it continues the work of ecumenism in obedience to the will of Christ. While dialogues flourish, ecumenical relations are sometimes strained by ambiguous language, the ordination of women by Episcopalians, inappropriate instances of eucharistic sharing, proselytism, and differing concepts of evangelization.

Cardinal Willebrands in his response clarified a number of the questions which were raised. The revised *Ecumenical Directory* which is now in preparation will be of great assistance to the bishops in their pastoral ministry when it is issued. Some of the bishops voiced their expectations in this regard.

Despite some problematic issues, which were discussed at some length and must be addressed in the future, Catholic-Jewish relations flourish uniquely in our nation.

Conclusion

One of the things that has most impressed me during this meeting—and I have heard others say the same thing—is the great commitment to and love for the Church on the part of all. It is this commitment and love that has prompted us all to speak, with candor and conviction, about the challenges facing the Church and how we might best address those challenges. Sometimes we are portrayed as being in a state of conflict or confrontation. A more accurate view is that we are men of faith, in love and united with the Lord, in communion with our Holy Father and with each other and all the bishops of the Church. Surely there are differences, as we heard during the many hours of discussion, but these differences stem from a single, burning desire: to teach and evangelize in the most effective way possible, given the cultural and societal realities of our time. It is only through such exchanges that we find the best way to fulfill our God-given responsibility.

During these days, our Holy Father has confirmed us in our faith. It is our task now to stand in solidarity with him and with one another as we continue the reflections we have begun and pursue the paths which are open to us. Such solidarity—rooted in faith and animated by mutual love and trust—will be a powerful sign to our people that there is indeed but "one Lord, one faith, one baptism." Such a sign will help to engender in them and in us a new sense of purpose, a new hope, a unity that transcends the diversities that characterize and enrich our lives. Many thanks, Holy Father, for giving us this opportunity.

Closing Address
by His Holiness John Paul II

Dear Brothers in the Episcopate,

For four days we have been together. We have prayed, reflected on, and discussed our ministry as successors of the apostles, called to be living signs of Jesus Christ: the compassionate Christ, the praying Christ, the faithful and contradicted Christ, the Christ who came "to preach the Gospel to the poor" (Mk 10:45). As our assembly draws to a close, I am sure that we share a great sense of gratitude to God for what this meeting has meant for us as pastors, individually and collectively, and for the life of the Church in the United States. Truly, Christ has been in our midst; the Holy Spirit has been our strength and guide; and we have done all things for the glory of the Father. Together we have experienced the joy which the psalm extolls: "How good and how pleasant it is, brothers dwelling in unity! . . . For there the Lord gives his blessing, life forever" (Ps 133:1, 3).

Our contact during these days has further educated us in the collegial spirit and given us a chance to express the communion and solidarity that unite us in Christ and in the Church. A first general conclusion which can be drawn is the usefulness of this type of gathering for understanding on questions or situations affecting the pastoral life of the Church in the various geographical and cultural spheres of her activity.

The central theme of our discussions in the general context of evangelization has been the "Bishop as Teacher of the Faith." It is not my intention here to review the important analyses made of the concrete cultural and social circumstances in which you are called to proclaim the gospel message as pastors of the Church in the United States. It will be my concern and yours, and the concern of our brother bishops, to continue this reflection on the relationship between the Christian message and the contexts in which it is preached and lived. At this time I refer briefly to the more personal and more basic question of the bishop's role as teacher of the faith as it springs from the consecration we received with the fullness of the sacrament of orders. Jesus' prayer for his disciples at the Last Supper calls us to consider the radical question of our responsibility for the truth: "[Father] . . . sanctify them in the truth; your word is truth. As you sent me into the world, so I have sent them into the world. And for their sake I consecrate myself, so that they also may be consecrated in truth" (Jn 17:17-19). As Peter in your midst, I must encourage and confirm you and your suffragans and the auxiliary bishops, and the particular churches over which you preside, in this consecration to the truth that is the Word of God, that is the Son of God made flesh for the salvation of all.

In essence, during these days we have been speaking about faith and the transmission of faith. Underlying our discussion at all times has been the question of the faith reflected in the particular churches of your nation, a faith alive in the laity, religious, and clergy who form, with the bishops, the Catholic Church in the United States. With my collaborators in the Roman Curia, I give thanks to God for the faith-filled history of the Church in your country, of which your saints are the most eloquent witnesses. The generous missionary spirit of your sons and daughters—religious, priests, and laity—has been and is being evidenced in many parts of the world.

You have reflected at length on the ways in which you can better carry out your pastoral service to the women and men religious of your dioceses, sustaining them in their demanding but extremely fruitful observance of the evangelical counsels. You have spoken of the immense contribution of individual religious and religious congregations to the life of the Church in your country, while at the same time recognizing that the state of religious life presents special problems and challenges which require your continuing attention. You have expressed your determination to pursue with responsibility and sensitivity your pastoral service in this regard.

Allow me to say a special word about the priests. In our discussion on their role as agents of evangelization, many spoke of the devotion and effectiveness of the priests in the United States. It was noted that in some ways they most directly bear the burden of the factors in your culture which clash with their mission to teach and evangelize. With you, I thank the priests of the United States for their ministry, for all they do to proclaim more effectively Jesus Christ as Lord. As you and your suffragan bishops gather with your priests for the Chrism Mass this year, please assure them of my gratitude, my affection, and blessing. You have brought them even closer to my heart during these days.

You have given much attention to the celebration of faith in the liturgy and the administration of the Church's sacraments, especially the sacrament of penance. In fact one of the first requirements of evangelization, one of the very first demands that faith makes on each person who wishes to embrace Christ, is penance or conversion. In the opening verses of St. Mark's gospel, Jesus himself presents a synthesis of this call to salvation with the words: "Repent and believe in the gospel" (Mk 1:15). To the bishops of Region V on their *Ad Limina* visits I suggested that "conversion as proclaimed by Christ is a whole program of life and pastoral action. It is the basis for an organic view of pastoral ministry because it is linked to all the great aspects of God's revelation" (May 31, 1988).

You have discussed conversion in its sacramental form and efficacy. One of the universal needs of the Church, which is also among the special requirements of the Church in the United States, is the restoration of the sacrament of penance and the renewal of its use (cf. *Reconciliatio et Penitentia*, 28). Such a renewal will have an important influence on families, the young, and on all the laity; its proper and frequent use can profoundly affect religious life, the fostering of vocations, the spiritual preparation of seminarians, and the ministry of our brother priests.

At this point we return to the difficulty which has surfaced time and time again in our discussions, the task of handing on the truths of the faith in a cultural context which questions the integrity and often the very existence of truth. Much of what has been discussed reflects this fundamental challenge to the contemporary Church as she seeks to evangelize. You have pointed to the many ways in which the various agents of evangelization might be helped to proclaim the truths of Scripture and tradition more effectively. I encourage you to give these suggestions serious consideration.

It is essential that the agents, and in the first place we the pastors, speak the true message, "the gospel of God, which he promised beforehand through his prophets in the holy Scriptures, the gospel concerning his Son . . . through whom we have received grace and apostleship to bring about the obedience of faith for the sake of his name among all the nations" (Rom 1:1-5). We are guardians of something given, and given to the Church universal; something which is not the result of reflection, however competent, on cultural and social questions of the day and is not merely the best path among many, but the one and only path to salvation: "there is no other name under heaven given among men by which we must be saved" (Acts 4:12). The people of God and those near and far must hear the name. We are all—you and I—bound to make an examination of conscience about how we are fulfilling the task, "lest the cross of Christ be emptied of its power" (1 Cor 1:17). The true measure of our success will consist in greater holiness, more loving service of those in need, and the advancement of truth and justice in every sphere of the life of your people and your country. As one of our brothers so rightly said: "Success cannot be the criterion or the condition of evangelization. The criterion and condition of evangelization must be fidelity to the mission."

Difficulties will not be lacking. What is important is that challenges or even opposition to the saving truth which the Church professes be met within the context of faith. Our Lord and Savior Jesus Christ in this and in all things points the way for us. Recall St. John's account of Jesus' teaching which the Church understands as revealing the Eucharist (cf. Jn 6). Peter's response then must be Peter's response today, a response spoken in the name of the apostles and their successors: "Lord, to whom shall we go? You have the words of eternal life" (Jn. 6:68).

In the final analysis, in evangelization we are concerned with proclaiming the truth of Jesus Christ and his Church, the truth that gives life, the truth that alone sets free. Jesus Christ reveals to us the truth who is God and the truth that is the totally free human person. The Lord speaks to us as we face our task when he says: "If you continue in my word, you are truly my disciples, and you will know the truth, and the truth will make you free" (Jn 8:32).

I am sure that in this meeting we have all become even more aware of the reasons for our certitude about our mission and its value for today's world. The source of our confidence is God himself. But we are also deeply encouraged by the holiness and willing service of so many of God's people: young and old, rich and poor, priests, religious, and laity. You will go back to particular churches which are spiritually rich and already possess the resources for a renewed evangelization. You will report to your brother bishops that the central theme which we discussed in brotherhood and love was the need to be found faithful in handing on what we ourselves have received (cf. 1 Cor 4:2); faithful in breaking the bread of truth and friendship with your priests; faithful in ensuring the full and solid formation of seminarians; faithful in ministering to the life and charism of religious; faithful in catechesis; faithful in encouraging the laity to take their proper and rightful place in the Church's life and mission; faithful in upholding the values of life and love in marriage and family life.

As I thank you and your brother bishops for the ministry you exercise with love and self-giving and encourage you to pursue further the reflections of these days, I invite the whole Church in the United States to live by faith in the Son of God, who loved us and gave himself for us (cf. Gal 2:20).

Through the intercession of the Blessed Virgin Mary and for the glory of the Most Blessed Trinity, may "the God of peace be with you all. Amen" (Rom 15:33).

Closing Address
by Archbishop John May

Most Holy Father, Brothers of the Roman Curia, Brothers from the United States, Dear Brothers All,

As we close this historic meeting with you here in Rome, all of us will return to America with greater love for you, Holy Father, greater appreciation for your collaboration in your service as universal pastor, and a renewed commitment to our own work as pastors, evangelists, and servants of our people. These have been most encouraging days for us, and we hope that we have shown you once again our total cooperation and loyalty.

We have most especially appreciated the generous time and full attention you have given to us during these days. Each one of us knows that you, Holy Father, and your fellow servants—all of those people—will return to desks piled high with work which was set aside while you shared your thoughts and impressions with us.

We thank all of you with all our hearts. It was a special blessing for us to concelebrate the Lord's sacrifice with you near the tomb of St. Peter this morning, where we prayed that we all might be perfect in unity.

Finally, on behalf of all the U.S. bishops, we thank their eminences, Cardinals Casaroli and Gantin, Archbishop Re, Dr. Navarro-Valls, and their staff for their careful attention to every detail in preparing and implementing this meeting. Our thanks also go to Cardinal Bernardin and our own pro-nuncio, Archbishop Laghi, for their work of preparation prior to our arrival.

We return home now, paraphrasing in our hearts the thought of blessed Peter, "Lord, it was good for us to be here."

Opening Statement at Telepress Conference (March 13, 1989)

Archbishop John May

Archbishop Quinn, Archbishop Kelly, and I returned last night from Rome. There, for the last four days, we have been meeting, along with 32 other cardinals and archbishops of the United States, with Pope John Paul II and 25 of his closest collaborators in the Roman Curia. The theme of these meetings has been evangelization in the American cultural context, with emphasis on the bishops' teaching role. We are grateful for the opportunity this morning, by means of this telepress conference, to bring the people of the United States a report on this meeting.

I believe that as a result of this meeting the bridge between Rome and the United States is stronger than it has ever been in recent memory. We feel that we have had the opportunity to speak with Rome of our successes and our concerns, to tell the stories of what we see and hear as we walk the streets of our land. Equally important, we feel that we have had the chance to listen—to hear the points of view of those whose concerns must revolve not simply around a single nation, but around the globe and the 850 million Catholics who people it. We, the archbishops of the United States, feel affirmed by these four days of meetings: We have a heightened sense that Pope John Paul and the members of the Curia understand our situation and support us in our work—that they recognize that it is no easy job to be a bishop, especially in America.

What was interesting to us was how often our own sketch of the backdrop against which we work matched the picture drawn by those with whom we spoke. Many of the same problems were mentioned by archbishops from the United States and members of the Curia: the exaggerated individualism, which frequently exalts personal satisfaction above the common good; the growing secularism of society, which ignores values that are permanent and even eternal; a moral relativism in which absolute values vanish; the consumerism of our day, with its fixation on building material kingdoms; and the mass media's glorification of sexual satisfaction as an end in itself, unrelated to persons and values.

America, of course, is not the only nation which suffers from these problems, and Rome knows this well. But Rome also knows that trends in America reach the rest of the world very quickly. So the common agenda of everyone in the room became this: how best to reach out with the message of the Gospel to a society battered by these countervailing forces—and especially how to reach out to all the people of the United States.

Clearly, there were some differences of perspective in the room, as might be expected in any gathering of five dozen such people, but these differences have to do with approach and not with doctrine. The Church's teaching is universal; the bishops of the United States work to support, defend, and promote that teaching as do the Curia officials in Rome.

Many of the factors that make America distinctive are the ones that make her great—the freedom of thought and expression, the pluralism of cultures and religions, the democratic spirit which values the opinion of each individual. America is a "marketplace society," where ideas have to sell themselves on their own intrinsic merit. That this would conflict at times with the hierarchical nature of the Church is not surprising. What we came to Rome to say (and it was received calmly and well) was that this spirit of America must influence our own approach in the United States. Though the teaching of the Church is one and universal, our approach in presenting this teaching must be custom-fitted to the United States.

Over and over again, through the course of four days, in both the formal presentations and the many hours of discussion, there was evident the great esteem which Pope John Paul and the Curia have for the Church in the United States—for the fidelity and zeal of our priests and religious; for the strong and growing involvement of the laity in the work of the Church; for the interaction of U.S. bishops with the great moral issues of our day as evidenced especially by our pastoral letters on war and peace and on the economy. We Roman Catholic archbishops are tremendously proud of Catholics in the United States, and Rome has told us clearly that this pride is well placed.

Speaking for myself—and I'm confident that I can speak here also for all the Americans involved in this meeting—this last week has been a profound spiritual experience. Never before have I had such a deep sense of the universal Church and of my own role in it. That sense of universality was evident in the meeting room, where there was no sense of one "team" pitted against another, but where people from five continents sat around a table and conversed about how best to bring the message of Jesus to one of the world's 170 nations. That universality—together with a sense of history— was evident perhaps even more dramatically on Saturday morning when the 60 participants in the meeting gathered with Pope John Paul around the tomb of St. Peter, the first pope, to celebrate in the Eucharist our common faith and constant unity.

Cardinal Bernardin told the press at the meeting's outset that this was not slated to be an action-oriented meeting. There was no plan, for example, to develop a consensus document or a set of specific resolutions. Yet certainly the meeting did have a result: the result is that stronger bonds have been forged between the Church in the United States and the Church universal. The ultimate question, of course, is still to be answered: whether this newfound strength will bring more and more people to a deeper commitment to Jesus Christ and to his work on earth.

Letter to the U.S. Bishops from His Holiness John Paul II

Dear Brothers in the Episcopate,

Following the recent meeting in the Vatican of the metropolitan archbishops of the United States with myself and members of the Roman Curia, and as the solemn feast of Easter draws near, I am happy to send you my warmest fraternal greetings in the love of our risen Lord and Savior Jesus Christ. The Church's annual celebration of the central mysteries of our faith—the passion, death, and resurrection of Jesus—is an appropriate time for us, the successors of the apostles, to renew in mind, heart, and action our commitment to one of the foremost tasks springing from our episcopal ordination: to be witnesses and teachers of the word of truth, the Gospel of our salvation (cf. Eph 1:13). The resurrection, in fact, is the preeminent sign of the power of the Gospel to save men and women in every age and in every place and culture. Indeed, the paschal mystery is the deepest source of our trust in our own ministry as bishops.

The encounter with the U.S. metropolitans provided an occasion for a most fruitful reflection and discussion on important aspects of the Church's evangelizing role in your country, which will offer valuable points of reference for your future ministry. It was also an intense experience of the abiding presence in our midst of the Holy Spirit, the divine counselor who guides us unto all truth (cf. Jn 16:13). The Eucharist which we celebrated at the tomb of the Prince of the Apostles symbolized in a powerful way the communion which united us in Christ and in the Church. There we gave thanks for the Church in the United States, for you the bishops, as well as for the priests, deacons, religious, and laity. We implored God's blessings upon your particular churches and on all those in need.

Rather than a list of specific conclusions, you who were present will convey to those whom you represented an increased awareness of the challenges that call the Church in the United States to proclaim ever more effectively the mystery of Christ. While yours is a culture with many positive values, it is at the same time, like everything human, marked by elements that need to be purified and uplifted by the saving message of the Gospel (cf. *Evangelii Nuntiandi*, 20). In this perspective, our task as pastors is to speak always the truth of Jesus Christ entrusted to the Church—that truth which gives life and which alone can set us free.

In our discussions, those ordained to the ministerial priesthood occupied a very significant place because of their unique role in building up and sustaining each local church and because of the love, understanding, and gratitude that all the bishops manifested in their regard. Bishops have a special ministry to priests, to encourage and support them. Justice and charity require that wise and careful attention be given to all aspects of their formation, life, and ministry. In this, as in every important ecclesial matter, it is imperative to study and implement the documents of the Second Vatican Council in all their richness and inspiration. I will pray for the priests of the United States in a special way at this week's Chrism Mass, as together we recommit ourselves to the demands of our common sacramental configuration with Christ.

My own part in the meeting corresponded to the requirements of the Petrine ministry of which I spoke during our gathering in Los Angeles in 1987, as not only a "global" service, reaching each particular church from "outside" as it were, but as belonging already to the essence of each particular church from "within" (cf. *Address to U.S. Bishops*, September 16, 1987, no. 4). It is of the greatest importance that in the full power of the Church's communion we continue to proclaim together Jesus Christ and his Gospel. In this way, we ourselves live fully, as successors of the apostles, the mystery of ecclesial communion. At the same time, through our ministry, we enable the faithful to enter ever more deeply into the Church's life of communion with the most Holy Trinity (cf. ibid.).

As we celebrate the glory of the risen Lord, I pray for each of you and for the whole Church in the United States. I give thanks to God for the profound *collegialitas effectiva et affectiva* that unites us in the mystery of Christ and his Church and which was clearly manifested in our recent meeting. I commend to the intercession of the Mother of God, Mary Immaculate, the continuing and urgent tasks and challenges of your teaching, sanctifying, and governing ministry. As a token of fraternal love and esteem, I gladly impart my apostolic blessing.

List of Meeting Participants

Vatican Officials

William Cardinal Baum
Prefect of the Congregation for Catholic Education

Agostino Cardinal Casaroli
Secretary of State

Luigi Cardinal Dadaglio
Grand Penitentiary

Roger Cardinal Etchegaray
President of the Pontifical Council for Justice and Peace
and President of the Pontifical Council "Cor Unum"

Angelo Cardinal Felici
Prefect of the Congregation for the Causes of Saints

Edouard Cardinal Gagnon
President of the Pontifical Council for the Family

Barnardin Cardinal Gantin
Prefect of the Congregation for Bishops

Jean Jerome Cardinal Hamer
Prefect of the Congregation for Institutes of
Consecrated Life and Societies of Apostolic Life

Antonio Cardinal Innocenti
Prefect of the Congregation for the Clergy

Simon Cardinal Lourdusamy
Prefect of the Congregation for the Oriental Churches

Eduardo Francisco Cardinal Pironio
President of the Ponticial Council for the Laity

Paul Cardinal Poupard
President of the Pontifical Council for Dialogue
with Non-Believers

Joseph Cardinal Ratzinger
Prefect of the Congregation for the Doctrine of the Faith

Achille Cardinal Silvestrini
Prefect of the Supreme Tribunal of the Apostolic Signatura

Eduardo Cardinal Martinez Somalo
Prefect of the Congregation for Divine Worship and
the Discipline of the Sacraments

Jozef Cardinal Tomko
Prefect of the Congregation for the Evangelization
of Peoples

Johannes Cardinal Willebrands
President of the Pontifical Council for Promoting
Christian Unity

Archbishop Fiorenzo Angelini
Pro-President of the Pontifical Council for
Pastoral Assistance to Health Care Workers

Archbishop Eduard Cassidy
Substitute of the Secretariat of State

Archbishop Giovanni Cheli
Pro-President of the Pontifical Council for the Pastoral
Care of Migrants and Itinerant People

Archbishop John Patrick Foley
President of the Pontifical Council for
Social Communications

Archbishop Pio Laghi
Apostolic Pro-Nuncio in the United States of America

Archbishop Giovanni Battista Re
Secretary of the Congregation for Bishops

Archbishop Justic Francis Rigali
President of the Pontifical Ecclesiastic Academy

Archbishop Angelo Sodano
Secretary of the Section for Relations with States
of the Secretariat of State

Hierarchy of the United States

Joseph Cardinal Bernardin
Archbishop of Chicago

James Cardinal Hickey
Archbishop of Washington, D.C.

Bernard Cardinal Law
Archbishop of Boston

John Cardinal O'Connor
Archbishop of New York

Edmund Cardinal Szoka
Archbishop of Detroit

Archbishop Anthony Bevilacqua
Archbishop of Philadelphia

Archbishop William Borders
Archbishop of Baltimore

Archbishop Patrick Flores
Archbishop of San Antonio

Archbishop Raymond Hunthausen
Archbishop of Seattle

Archbishop Francis Hurley
Archbishop of Anchorage

Archbishop Thomas Kelly, OP
Archbishop of Louisville

Archbishop Stephen Kocisko
Archbishop of Pittsburgh (Byzantine)

Archbishop Daniel Kucera, OSB
Archbishop of Dubuque

Archbishop William Levada
Archbishop of Portland in Oregon

Archbishop Oscar Lipscomb
Archbishop of Mobile

Archbishop Roger Mahony
  Archbishop of Los Angeles

Archbishop Eugene Marino, SSJ
  Archbishop of Atlanta

Archbishop John May
  Archbishop of St. Louis

Archbishop Theodore McCarrick
  Archbishop of Newark

Archbishop Edward McCarthy
  Archbishop of Miami

Archbishop Thomas Murphy
  Coadjutor Archbishop of Seattle

Archbishop Edward O'Meara
  Archbishop of Indianapolis

Archbishop Daniel Pilarczyk
  Archbishop of Cincinnati

Archbishop John Quinn
  Archbishop of San Francisco

Archbishop John Roach
  Archbishop of St. Paul and Minneapolis

Archbishop Joseph Ryan
  Archbishop of Military Services USA

Archbishop Charles Salatka
  Archbishop of Oklahoma City

Archbishop Robert Sanchez
  Archbishop of Santa Fe

Archbishop Francis Schulte
  Archbishop of New Orleans

Archbishop Daniel Sheehan
  Archbishop of Omaha

Archbishop J. Francis Stafford
  Archbishop of Denver

Archbishop Ignatius Strecker
Archbishop of Kansas City in Kansas

Archeparch Stephen Sulyk
Archeparch of Philadelphia (Ukranian)

Archbishop Rembert Weakland, OSB
Archbishop of Milwaukee

Archbishop John Whealon
Archbishop of Hartford

Bishop William Keeler
Bishop of Harrisburg

Reverend Robert Lynch (Observer)
General Secretary, National Conference of Catholic
Bishops and United States Catholic Conference